Ethics and the Good Teacher

Ethics and the Good Teacher brings together reviews of existing literature and analysis of empirical data from three research projects conducted by the Jubilee Centre for Character and Virtues – *The Good Teacher, Schools of Virtue* and *Teacher Education* – to explore the ethical dimensions of the teaching profession.

The book is premised on the idea that what constitutes a "good" teacher involves more than technical skills and subject knowledge. Understood as a professional activity, teaching involves an important ethical dimension, a fact that has come under increased scrutiny – and some would argue increased threat – over recent years as education and schooling have become shaped by market logic and accountability.

Addressing the influence of personal and professional character on teachers and teaching, and containing clear implications for policy, practice and research, this book will be of great interest to teachers and other professionals working in education settings, as well as those working in education policy. It will also appeal to academics, undergraduate students and postgraduate students researching the teaching profession and ethics/morality in education more generally.

Andrew Peterson is Professor of Character and Citizenship Education and Deputy Director of the Jubilee Centre for Character and Virtues at the University of Birmingham, UK.

James Arthur is Professor of Education and Civic Engagement and Director of the Jubilee Centre for Character and Virtues at the University of Birmingham, UK.

Character and Virtue Within the Professions

Series Editors

James Arthur, *Professor of Education and Civic Engagement and Director of the Jubilee Centre for Character and Virtues at the University of Birmingham, UK.*

Andrew Peterson, *Professor of Character and Citizenship Education and Deputy Director of the Jubilee Centre for Character and Virtues at the University of Birmingham, UK.*

The principal objective of the series is to highlight the interplay between practitioners' personal character and the ethical dimensions of their professional domain. Each book will explore the specific ethical dimensions of the given profession at hand, including the relationship between professionals' individual character virtues and their working environments. In a time when cultures of managerialism, auditing, performance metrics and commercial success are seemingly increasing, this series attempts to re-focus the professions towards the ethical and societal origins that each profession intends to serve. Underpinned by perspectives of philosophy, psychology and sociology, each book will offer practitioners fresh viewpoints about how their character and professional context can influence their professional practice.

Books in the series include:

Ethics and the Good Teacher
Character in the Professional Domain
Andrew Peterson with James Arthur

For more information about this series, please visit: www.routledge.com/Character-and-Virtue-Within-the-Professions/book-series/CVP

Ethics and the Good Teacher

Character in the Professional Domain

Andrew Peterson with James Arthur

LONDON AND NEW YORK

First published 2021
by Routledge
2 Park Square, Milton Park, Abingdon, Oxon OX14 4RN

and by Routledge
52 Vanderbilt Avenue, New York, NY 10017

Routledge is an imprint of the Taylor & Francis Group, an informa business

British Library Cataloguing-in-Publication Data
A catalogue record for this book is available from the British Library

Library of Congress Cataloging-in-Publication Data
Names: Peterson, Andrew, 1976– author. | Arthur, James, 1957– author.
Title: Ethics and the good teacher: character in the
professional domain / Andrew Peterson with James Arthur.
Description: Abingdon, Oxon; New York, NY: Routledge, 2020. |
Series: Character and virtue within the professions |
Includes bibliographical references and index.
Identifiers: LCCN 2020009596 (print) | LCCN 2020009597 (ebook) |
ISBN 9780367335885 (hardback) | ISBN 9780429320699 (ebook)
Subjects: LCSH: Teachers—Professional ethics. |
Teaching—Moral and ethical aspects. | Moral education.
Classification: LCC LB1779 .P47 2020 (print) | LCC LB1779 (ebook) |
DDC 174/.9372—dc23
LC record available at https://lccn.loc.gov/2020009596
LC ebook record available at https://lccn.loc.gov/2020009597

ISBN: 978-0-367-33588-5 (hbk)
ISBN: 978-0-429-32069-9 (ebk)

Typeset in Times New Roman
by codeMantra

Contents

Acknowledgements

This book is the first in a series of texts that will examine *Character and Virtues in the Professions*. Each book in the series will be dedicated to a specific profession and will bring together reviews of existing literature and sources of empirical data – including data collected in various projects by the Jubilee Centre for Character and Virtues – to provide new insights for both pre- and in-service professionals, as well as acting as an educational resource to inform future professional decision-making and practice.

As we make clear from the outset, this book draws extensively on data and analysis from three projects conducted and reported on by the Jubilee Centre that were all led by the Centre's Director, James Arthur. For this reason, we owe our sincere gratitude to those colleagues whose data collection, analysis, recommendations and overall insight on the three projects, including in their resulting reports, has made this book possible. In particular, our thanks and acknowledgements go to Kristján Kristjánsson, Sandra Cooke, Emma Brown, David Carr, Stephen Earl, Tom Harrison, Emily Burn, Francisco Moller, Michael Fullard and Paul Watts. We are also grateful to our colleagues at Routledge – in particular Anna Clarkson and Sarah Tuckwell – for their interest and support in this series and book.

James Arthur
Andrew Peterson

Introduction

Introduction

This book, and the studies contained within it, is premised on the idea that what constitutes a 'good' teacher necessarily involves more than technical skills and subject knowledge. Although the capacities to manage educational environments and to understand and convey core disciplinary concepts and skills are important components of good teaching, they are not all that good teaching comprises. Understood as a professional activity, teaching involves an important ethical dimension, a fact that has come under increased scrutiny – and some would argue increased threat – over recent years as education and schooling have become shaped by market logic and accountability.

Recognising that teaching involves an ethical dimension and represents an essentially moral undertaking is one thing; explicating the precise nature of this ethical and moral dimension is another, and altogether more difficult and contentious, matter. While a number of researchers (as we examine in later chapters) have sought to re-state and reclaim the moral basis of teaching as a professional activity, much work remains in understanding how the ethical work of the teacher is understood and approached in practice. Since its inception in 2012, the Jubilee Centre for Character and Virtues has conducted numerous studies that have sought the views, perceptions and explanations of teachers themselves in order to interrogate and explore the ethical dimensions of teaching in England. In this book, we draw on three of these studies in particular, each led by the Centre's Director, James Arthur. While we add some additional analysis to the findings, this book draws extensively on the respective reports produced by the projects.

The main study drawn upon – titled *The Good Teacher* (Arthur et al., 2015a) – aimed to understand the characteristics of a good teacher in a moral, ethical and professional sense. In the chapters which follow, we supplement an analysis of data from *The Good Teacher* project with connected data from other projects undertaken by the Jubilee Centre that have focused on the role of teachers in developing pupils character, including *Schools of Virtue* (Arthur et al., 2017) and *Teacher Education* (Arthur et al., 2018a). The Centre's work on the ethical dimensions of teaching as a profession has also been detailed in various articles and books published by Centre members that focus both on teaching itself (for example, Kristjánsson, 2013, 2015b; Cooke and Carr, 2014; Arthur et al., 2016; Morris and Ryan, 2016; Harrison and Walker, 2018; Harrison, Sanderse and Cooke, 2019) and on the professions more widely (for example, Arthur et al, 2015b, 2019a, 2019b; Harrison and Khatoon, 2017; Kristjánsson et al., 2017a, 2017b; Arthur, Walker, and Thoma, 2018b).

The aim of this introductory chapter is two-fold. First, we provide summary details of the main projects drawn upon in our analysis. For reasons of space and concision, here we present an overview of the main aims, research questions and methods for each of these projects. The detailed aims, research questions and methods of each of this project can be found on the Jubilee Centre's website and in the various reports published from each of the projects. Second, we set out the structure of the book, including the focus and broad content of each of the chapters that follow.

The projects

The Good Teacher project

The Good Teacher project was a three-year study, in Great Britain, involving students (referred to as *Student Teachers* throughout), teachers who had recently graduated from their pre-service teacher education programme (referred to throughout as *Newly Qualified Teachers*, or NQTs) and practicing teachers with at least five years of teaching experience (referred to as *Experienced Teachers*). The project was designed to deepen understanding of the place of virtues and character in the education, training and practice of teachers. As stated in the final report (Arthur et al., 2015a: 10), the overarching aims of *The Good Teacher* project were to:

- understand what the characteristics of a *good* teacher are, in the moral, ethical and professional sense of the word. The project aimed, therefore, to explore those morally relevant aspects of

teachers' professional lives that are often neither highlighted in mainstream educational discourse nor necessarily found in professional standards;
- explore the conditions under which teachers felt able to exercise practical wisdom for the good of their students, what helped them to do so and what they considered to be barriers to wise and virtuous practice; and
- examine how teacher education and continued professional development can be organised to support good teaching through the development of teachers' moral character.

The main research questions which guided the project were:

- What are the important character strengths, or virtues, needed for good teaching?
- What are the reported character strengths, or virtues, held by today's teachers?
- How do character strengths, or virtues, influence teaching in practice?
- How do regulatory and organisational structures facilitate good teaching?
- How might initial and continued professional education contribute to the further development of good teaching?

The project's research design incorporated self-reporting measures of personal and professional character, as well as ethical dilemmas and extensive interviews with teachers at different stages of their careers. Two main data collection tools were used: an online questionnaire and semi-structured interviews.

The online questionnaire consisted of five sections (four for starting undergraduates), surveying, in order:

1. Respondents' views on their own character (a list of 24 character strengths, derived from the *Values in Action* inventory [Peterson and Seligman, 2004; Peterson and Park, 2009], from which respondents were asked to identify the six that 'best describe the sort of person you are');
2. Respondents' responses to a set of professional dilemmas (six dilemmas which explore the role of virtues and values in decision making, using scenarios and a scoring system created by, and piloted with, an expert panel[1] of over 40 practitioners and educators);

3 Respondents' views on the character of the 'ideal' teacher (the list of 24 character strengths presented again with respondents asked to choose the six which they thought best described an 'ideal' teacher). This was followed by an open question asking respondents to write about a teacher they had met who showed many of these character strengths;
4 Respondents' views regarding their work or study environment (not included for starting undergraduates). This section used and adapted questions from a Europe-wide workplace survey [Eurofound, 2012] with additional questions on ethical issues in the workplace; and
5 A set of demographic questions, followed by an open question asking respondents to describe their reasons for entering the teaching profession (Arthur et al., 2015a: 13)

Dilemmas were used as they (a) promise to offer a credible way to gain an insight into moral functioning and development and (b) can ideally be designed so as to activate more than simply moral reasoning skills (Kristjánsson, 2015a, Chap. 3). Nevertheless, responses to dilemmas serve as an indication, rather than guarantee, of action or understanding of moral sensitivity in a real, particular situation. They do not, in and by themselves, *measure* virtue, nor do any such definitive measures exist elsewhere, but when combined with data from interviews and self-reports, they may contribute to an overall understanding of virtue in professional practice. Analysis of the dilemma data is the subject of Chapter 4, and a summary of the content and associated virtues for each of the dilemmas can be found in Appendix Two. The questionnaire consisted of four or five sections, depending on career stage. Responses were examined for errors, and only those with complete dilemma responses were included in the working dataset. The first priority for data analysis consisted of compiling descriptive statistics of answers, by career stage, to allow for early comparisons. Initial stage data analysis was then summarised. To analyse the ethical dilemmas section, a series of tests using SPSS, including two way analyses of variance (ANOVAs), and appropriate post hoc analyses were conducted to see where any differences of statistical significance lay (Arthur et al., 2015a: 13).

Semi-structured interviews were held with participants from each of the three career stages – Student Teachers, NQTs and Experienced Teachers – in order to interrogate the three main research questions. The interviews included questions around reasons for choice of career, the characteristics of a good teacher, factors that can help or hinder being that kind of professional, views on the influence of character on everyday professional practice, the influence of the Teachers'

Standards and the influence of education and training in developing the strengths necessary for good professional practice. For interviews with Teacher Educators, a separate set of questions was devised. These concentrated on their role in educating future teachers, their view of a good professional in their field, how this had changed in the course of their career, how students were assessed for entry, whether the character strengths required change and why, what informs their teaching in relation to the virtues and how Initial Teacher Education (ITE) might be developed. The majority of interviews with Student Teachers were conducted in person. For participants in the other two career stages, where in-person interviews were not possible, telephone interviews were undertaken. All Teacher Educator interviews were conducted in person. Audio tapes were transcribed with records returned to participants for member checking to allow for amendments. Analysis of interview data was thematic, using a constant comparison (Glaser and Strauss, 1967) within a modified framework approach (Ritchie and Spencer, 1994). Data from the interviews were analysed independently by project team members and codes developed according to the data. Codes were created both horizontally (by coding each interview as a stand-alone narrative) and vertically (by scanning across the data for specific terms) and then developed into categories and themes. Categories were refined and coding reviewed throughout the process using NVIVO software (Arthur et al., 2015a).

Project participants for the study were drawn from a number of universities engaged in ITE (*Student Teachers* and *NQTs*), and encompassed primary and secondary routes across a range of subject specialisms. *Experienced Teachers* were drawn from universities' mentor networks, together with help from known teachers who sought their head teacher's permission and forwarded the email to colleagues in their schools. The participants to be interviewed were chosen purposively. Questionnaire respondents were asked to indicate their willingness to be interviewed, and a member of the research team then made initial contact with the interviewee via the provided email address or telephone number and arranged a suitable date and time. The total number of participants, by career stage, is presented in Table 0.1. In its final analysis, *The Good Teacher* project drew upon 546 questionnaires and 95 interviews completed by Student Teachers, NQTs and Experienced Teachers in a variety of geographical, educational and professional settings in Great Britain, and at differing stages of their careers. At the time the report was written, much of the existing research elsewhere had focused on teachers' beliefs at particular stages of their careers, rather than comparisons *between* stages (Barrett et al., 2012).

Table 0.1 Total Number of Participants, by Career Stage

Career stage	*Interviews conducted*	*Questionnaires completed*
Student Teachers	25	235
NQTs	32	181
Experienced Teachers	26	130
Teacher Educators	12	n/a
Total	95	546

Limitations and ethical considerations

As stated in *The Good Teacher* project's final report (Arthur et al., 2015a: 15), the sample for *The Good Teacher* project relied on the willing participation both of gatekeepers (primarily course leaders) in the participating institutions and subsequently on the consent of those who responded to the questionnaire and, for some, the interviews. It should also be recognised that some participants in the project had a keen interest in the area and may have had particularly strong views, either positive or negative, on the subject matter. In addition, any study of professional ethics, virtues and values assumes, implicitly or explicitly, a certain understanding of how professionals make ethical judgements and implement them in practice. Professional practice is highly situational – it depends on the organisational, personal and social context at a given moment in time. Thus, to condense highly complex, dependent dilemmas into a research exercise is inevitably going to offer only one limited perspective. The project sought to challenge this by the triangulation of methods between the questionnaire and interviews so that key messages could be compared.

There are also several, more specific limitations associated with the research methods used, particularly in the self-report aspects of the design. Self-reporting is subject to inherent problems: self-deception biases, where respondents may see themselves as something other than they actually are in practice; social-desirability biases, or the tendency for participants to answer questions in ways that they believe will be viewed favourably by others; and self-confirmation biases where people respond to information in ways that confirm their beliefs, and discard information that contradicts those beliefs. A further potential problem lies in so-called 'demand characteristics', where participants try to work out the aim of the study and answer in ways to support those aims. There is also controversy over the use of ethical dilemmas as a tool for gauging moral performance. Some theorists still insist that such tools only measure (at best) moral reasoning, rather than giving any indication of overall moral functioning. Other theorists are more optimistic regarding such testing, seeing it as tapping into grand 'moral schemas' and therefore reaching beyond mere formal reasoning processes or skills (Kristjánsson, 2015a).

The Good Teacher project was granted initial, formal ethical approval by the University of Birmingham Ethics Committee, with subsequent modifications being approved as the design developed. All participants were provided information about the project prior to gaining their consent, and understood their commitment to the project, including the right to withdraw or modify their contribution at any point up to data analysis. Comprehensive consent forms were signed in duplicate once appropriate explanations and information sheets had been offered. Data were stored electronically in password-protected servers, and transcriptions were anonymised to protect participants' identities (Arthur et al., 2015a).

The Teacher Education project

The Jubilee Centre's *Teacher Education* project (ongoing at the time of writing) explores how teachers are prepared and supported to meet the moral and ethical demands of their roles. The overall project investigates the following research questions:

- How do pre-service and in-service programmes of teacher training prepare teachers to educate for character and virtue in the classroom?
- How do we best prepare new and experienced teachers to engage with the positive character formation of their students and of their peers?
- What are the most effective methods for educating and supporting teachers, at various stages of their career, to effectively fulfil their roles as character educators?
- What are the enablers and barriers to CPD programmes placing character education at the heart of their vision and practice?

The aspect of the project we draw upon in this book was designed to examine understandings of the place of character and virtues in the education, training and teaching practice of student teachers in primary and secondary school education. As set out in the project's interim report (Arthur et al., 2018a), the research involved student teachers from two UK universities offering a one-year post-graduate

ITE qualification in the form of a Post-Graduate Certificate in Education, or equivalent. The research project has captured the views of student teachers both at an early stage of training and at the end of their one-year ITE programme. Recognising the complexity of the issues, and seeking to expand upon previous research, multiple methods were used to collect data. The research therefore included a literature review and an analysis of profession-specific literature; two voluntary, paper-based surveys – one conducted with student teachers towards the start of the ITE programme (initial survey) and one conducted with the same student teachers in the final week of their ITE programme (post survey); voluntary completion of a reflective journal; and semi-structured interviews with a selection of participants who volunteered after completing the reflective journal. In this book, we draw on aspects of the preliminary research findings and discussions from the initial survey and post survey responses to extend and further illuminate the more extensive findings from *The Good Teacher* project.

The two universities involved in the *Teacher Education* project were identified through opportunistic sampling. In order to provide a balanced sample it was ensured that participants in both universities were drawn from both primary and secondary training settings, across a range of subjects. Essential to the study was the co-operation and participation of these universities: with the agreement of teacher educators at the chosen universities, members of the research team attended lectures at the earliest convenient dates from the start of the ITE programmes. Student teachers voluntarily completed the initial survey and then received an extended lecture on character education delivered by the research team. Members of the research team returned to both universities in the final week of the ITE programmes to administer the voluntary post survey (Arthur et al., 2018a). Table 0.2 provides an overview of the number of participants for each survey.

Table 0.2 The Total Number of Student Teacher Participants

	Initial survey responses	*Post survey responses*	*No of participants who completed both surveys*
University A Primary	92	90	70
University B Primary	123	119	100
University A Secondary	137	135	103
University B Secondary	180	149	113
Total	579	520	386

The initial and post surveys comprised the following sections:

A Respondents' views on **reflective practice**: Respondents were asked to define the term 'reflective practice' within the context of the teaching profession, to share their habits of reflection and to offer their views on the importance of reflecting on character within the teaching profession;
B Respondents' views on **character education**: Respondents were asked about their familiarity with the term 'character education', to define this and to offer their views on the importance of character within the teaching profession;
C Respondents' views on their own **personal character strengths**: A list of 24 character strengths, taken from the Jubilee Centre's *A Framework for Character Education in Schools* (2017) (see Figure 0.1), was presented and respondents were asked to rate, on a scale from 1 to 7, how well each character strength described them (7 being the strongest). Respondents were then asked to choose and rank the six character strengths which best described their own personal character;
D Respondents' views on the **character strengths of a 'good' teacher:** Using the same list of character strengths, respondents were asked to rate, on a scale from 1 to 7, how well each character strength described a 'good' teacher (7 being the strongest). Respondents were then asked to choose and rank the six character strengths which best described a 'good' teacher;
E Respondents' **experiences of character education during ITE** (post survey only): Respondents were asked for their views regarding the impact and style of training provided by the Jubilee Centre and their ITE programme in regard to character education, and their experiences of character education whilst on placement schools;
F A set of demographic questions (Arthur et al, 2018a).

The Jubilee Centre's *A Framework for Character Education in Schools* (2017) presents the Building Blocks of Character. This proposes four domains of virtue, from which the 24 virtues used in this research were taken (six virtues from each domain): intellectual, moral, civic and performance. In the *Student Teacher* project these virtues are referred to as character strengths.

Responses from the initial survey and post survey were entered into an Excel spreadsheet where they were cleaned and filtered, with only student teachers who completed both the initial survey and post survey included in the final data analysis. Subsequently, the data was

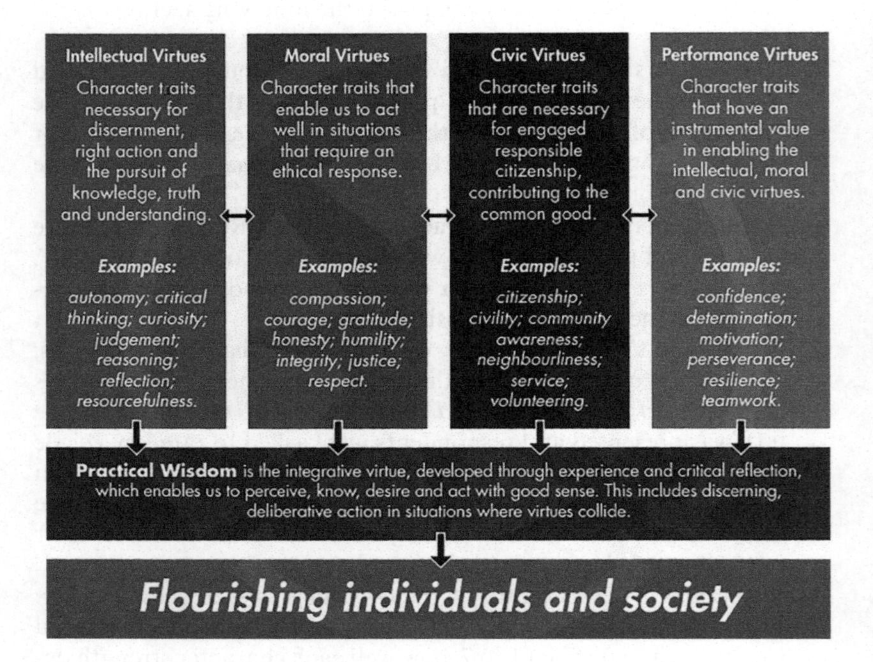

Figure 0.1 The Building Blocks of Character.

exported into SPSS version 24 to conduct the analysis. Frequency distributions of ordinal variables were compared using Pearson's chi square test. McNemar's test of marginal homogeneity was used to test differences on paired nominal data such as the initial survey to post survey changes on dichotomous variables. Finally, paired sample T tests were carried out to compare means between the two time points. When character strengths were ranked, a score was calculated to capture the magnitude of the selection made. In the top six rankings section, percentages refer to the proportion of the overall total score (Arthur et al., 2018a).

Limitations and ethical considerations

Similarly to *The Good Teacher* project, it is recognised that some of those choosing to take part in the *Teacher Education* project will have had a keen interest in the subject and may have had particularly strong views, either positive or negative, on the subject matter. The choice of sample means that conclusions drawn from the survey cannot be assuredly generalised to the whole population. Again, as with *The Good Teacher* project, there are also a number of more specific limitations associated with the self-report aspects of the design. Self-reporting is subject to inherent problems: self-deception biases[2]; social-desirability biases[3] and self-confirmation biases.[4] Responses may also have been affected by so-called 'demand characteristics', where participants try to work out the aim of the study and answer in ways to support those aims. The *Teacher Education* project was granted initial ethical approval by the University of Birmingham Ethics Committee, with subsequent modifications being approved as the design developed. The research team were conscious of their responsibilities to all participants to ensure they understood their commitment to the project and the right to withdraw or modify their contribution at any point up to the commencement of data analysis. Comprehensive consent forms were signed once appropriate explanations and information had been offered (Arthur et al., 2018a).

The Schools of Virtue project

As explained in its final report, The *Schools of Virtue* (Arthur et al., 2017: 6) study focussed on three schools in Birmingham that have been inspired by the Jubilee Centre's *A Framework for Character Education in Schools* (2017) and which have intentionally placed an emphasis on developing their pupils' character. The three schools were the University of Birmingham School, Nishkam High School, and St. Brigid's Catholic Primary School. An underpinning intention of the project was to appreciate that there is no set and static 'blueprint' for how schools develop character education. Given each individual school is different and has to take into account various contextual factors, every school needs to envision their own implementation of character education. As noted by Seider (2012: 220–222), the 'copying and pasting' of character education programmes within an existing school culture is unlikely to be successful. On this basis, the *Schools of Virtue* project sought to explore the practical steps the three schools had taken to implement character education in response to their own context.

Drawing on data from teaching staff and pupils, the *Schools of Virtue* study utilised a case study design. Purposive sampling was used to select the three schools on the basis that they each prioritised character education. While each was based in the Birmingham area, the three schools provided a range of contexts in which character education was implemented, both in terms of the catchment areas served and educational settings. The study employed mixed methods to allow for methodological triangulation, with both qualitative and quantitative methods employed through the use of interviews with teaching staff, group interviews with pupils, and a survey of pupils. When the data were analysed, a greater emphasis was placed on the qualitative data as these allowed a more extensive exploration of the context in which the school operates, along with the perceptions of the ways that character education has been implemented across the three schools.

In this book, we draw on the data obtained from the interviews with teaching staff, though information on the full methods and data collected from pupils can be found in the project report (Arthur et al., 2017). Semi-structured interviews with teaching staff were held across the three schools. A convenience approach to sampling was used whereby teaching staff were invited to participate by their schools; interviews with teaching staff took place between July 2016 and February 2017. Schools were asked to ensure that a mix of teaching staff were available to be interviewed according to the subject they teach, their gender and level of teaching experience. Questions focused on teachers' perceptions of the implementation and perceived influence of character education within the school. Questions also asked whether there were barriers and enablers which either helped or hindered the progression of character education within the school. The semi-structured nature of the interviews ensured flexibility so that the researchers were able to respond to the participants' comments.

All interviews were recorded and transcribed, with subsequent thematic analysis undertaken using the NVivo 11 software package. As an initial stage, the researchers familiarised themselves with the data, and interview transcriptions were coded with *a priori* themes established in the evaluation framework within the Centre's *Character Education: Evaluation Handbook for Schools* (Harrison, Arthur and Burn, 2016), as it was identified that these themes would encompass the breadth of character education. Such themes included: school ethos, culture and vision; curriculum; learning outside the classroom; whole school community and community links. These themes and related codes were then reviewed and refined and further emergent coding allowed sub-themes to be incorporated which developed a more comprehensive coding dictionary[5] (Arthur et al., 2017).

Limitations and ethical considerations

In order to explore the influence of character education, it was necessary for the *Schools of Virtue* study to work with those schools which were already focussed on the development and implementation of character education. Consequently, it was not possible to draw comparisons between those schools which have focussed on character education and those which have not. It should be noted, too, that two of the schools were faith schools; with St. Brigid's being a Catholic Primary School and Nishkam High School defining itself as a multi-faith school. The focus on faith within these two schools has not contradicted the development of the neo-Aristotelian lens which has informed the *Schools of Virtue* study. As argued by Arthur (2003: 53), character education within a Christian context can be understood in terms of a developmental model in which moral training is centred on both knowing and doing the good. Ethical approval was granted for the design of the *Schools of Virtue* study by the University of Birmingham Ethics Committee. In each of the three schools, a senior member of staff consented to the participation of their school. Subsequently, for each stage of the research, participants were provided with information sheets and consent or opt-out forms. Parents also provided their informed consent for their children to participate in interviews. Each of the three schools agreed to be named in the report. Teaching staff were guaranteed confidentiality, although they were informed that due to their schools being named in resulting publications, it may be the case that their comments could be attributed to their participation (Arthur et al., 2017).

The structure of this book

Following this introduction, the book comprises four main chapters and a conclusion which contains a summary of the main findings, recommendations and areas for further research. Chapter 1 presents a brief review of current literature in the wider field of professional ethics. Arguing that the ethical is central to what is meant by a 'profession', the chapter introduces the recent turn to virtues and character within literature on the professions, in particular the focus on *phronesis* (practical wisdom). In this context, the Jubilee Centre's *Building Blocks of Professional Practice* is also introduced. In Chapter 2, attention turns to the ethical nature of teaching and the teacher. Here we contend that, as with professions more generally, the ethical forms a fundamental component of what it is that constitutes the 'good' teacher. Surveying current literature in the field, the chapter also highlights some impacts on the ethical teacher of increased marketisation and instrumentalism within education.

In Chapters 3 and 4, data from the three projects introduced above is presented and analysed. In Chapter 3, this data concerns teacher motivations, how teachers conceive their role in developing young people's character and preparing teachers for this role. Data is presented which found that general notions of character and 'making a difference to the lives of children' form an important part of what motivates entrants to the profession. In addition, across the main three studies on which this book draws, teachers at various career stages have reported that they do view themselves as having an important role to play in pupils' character development. Yet, evidence from the projects also suggests that as teachers progress in their careers this role in character development becomes focused increasingly on performance rather than moral virtues.

In Chapter 4, we present and discuss data that examines how teachers at various stages of their career – Student Teacher, Newly Qualified Teacher and Experienced Teacher – conceive their own personal character strengths and those character strengths they identify with the 'ideal' or 'good' teacher. In addition, drawing on data collected through *The Good Teacher* project, we present analysis of responses to a series of ethical dilemmas given by teachers at various stages of their career. Analysis of the dilemma data found that while the majority of teachers can confidently apply moral virtues when making professional decisions, there are some situations where this is challenging (particularly in situations where virtues conflict). Data analysis also suggests some significant differences in response based on career stage and gender. The book closes with *Conclusions, Recommendations and Further Research.*

While empirical studies on moral education in UK schools remain rather limited in scope and extent, there has clearly been a renewed focus on the moral role of teachers in recent years within academia, government policy and schools (Hand, 2018; Hinds, 2019; OfSTED, 2019b). As a leading contributor to these debates, since its inception the Jubilee Centre for Character and Virtues has worked with a range of colleagues and organisations to support, investigate, distil and celebrate character education in schools. A central element of this work has been to examine the nature of teaching as a profession and, more specifically, the moral role of the teacher. Our intention in the pages that follow is to bring together data, analysis, findings and conclusions from the three projects introduced above in order to consolidate and share with new audiences what our projects have revealed about teaching and teachers and to open up areas for further investigation that might shape the research trajectory over the coming years.

Notes

1 The process by which the Expert Panel was formed, and its role in the research, can be found in Appendix 1.
2 A self-deception bias is where one sees oneself as something other than one is in practice.
3 A social-desirability bias is the tendency for participants to answer questions in ways that they believe will be viewed favourably by others.
4 A self-confirmation bias is where people respond to information in ways that confirm their beliefs and discard information that contradicts those beliefs.
5 The coding dictionary can be seen in the Online Appendices at www.jubileecentre.ac.uk/schoolsofvirtue.

1 The professions and character

Introduction

Whether inspired by a desire to justify an occupation's status as a profession (teaching and social work, for example) or by the need to reassert precisely what lies at the heart of a long-standing profession in the wake of public concerns about standards (nursing and law, for example), the related questions of what constitutes a profession and what constitutes professional practice have received a great deal of attention over recent years. A core concern within this literature on the professions has been to highlight and seek to understand the ethical basis of professions, whether generally or specifically. Professions are deemed inherently ethical occupations because, and more so than other occupations, they place high moral demands on the conduct of workers. Indeed, these ethical and moral demands – which include care, integrity, fairness and diligence – are often viewed as *the defining* feature of many professions, including medicine, law and teaching, reminding us that professions are ultimately concerned with *human* actions and interactions. Aslo, and as Oakley and Cocking (2001) assert, the focus of professional work is typically the provision of goods – such as health, education and justice – that are fundamental to flourishing individuals and societies. Yet, and as various professional 'scandals' over the last 20 years have evidenced, every profession – and by extension professional – faces ethical challenges and dilemmas. Indeed, the very ethical nature of the professions entails that public mistrust and criticism results when conduct falls below expected or stated standards (Blond, Antonacopoulou and Pabst, 2015).

In order to examine the ethical nature of professions and the ethical dilemmas experienced by professionals, since its inception the Jubilee Centre has undertaken a number of empirical studies examining character, virtues and the professions. Some of these studies have concentrated on the professions generally (Arthur et al., 2019a), while others have focused in on specific professions: law (Arthur et al., 2014), medical practice (Arthur et al., 2015b), education (Arthur et al., 2015a), business (Kristjánsson et al., 2017a), nursing (Kristjánsson et al., 2017b) and the British Army (Arthur et al., 2018b). More recently, through its project *Practical Wisdom and Professional Practice: Integration and Intervention*, the Centre is building on this research within these professions to examine particular commonalities and differences across professions and professionals (Arthur et al., 2019a).

The purpose of this first chapter is to provide an initial survey of the existing literature on the professions. The first section considers briefly what constitutes a profession in general terms, before turning to the more specific ethical dimensions of professional activity. It does so in light of the now widespread trend towards managerialism, accountability and efficiency that has been witnessed across professions in a number of countries over the last 30 years. In the second section, attention moves to consider the value of a virtue-based account of professional ethics. In this section we draw on the Jubilee Centre's neo-Aristotelian approach to virtues and character in order to argue that professional ethics not only involves, but also transcends, reliance on rules and duties, thereby requiring professionals to act with professional wisdom and judgement.

What constitutes a profession?

While definitions of what constitutes a profession abound, certain features seem to be generally, if not universally, accepted (see, for example, Carr, 1999). These are that:

- A profession is a paid occupation;
- A profession requires formal qualifications, a high level of education and a prolonged period of training/induction;
- A professional possesses high level theoretical and practical expertise in a given discipline;
- A profession provides a public service;
- A profession is, and professionals are, held in high esteem within society;
- A professional acts with integrity, care, honesty and trust, exhibiting a level of professional autonomy and judgement;
- Professional ethics is guided by a code of conduct specific to that profession.

The Australian Council of Professions,[1] which captures each of the features above, define a 'Profession' as:

> a disciplined group of individuals who adhere to ethical standards and who hold themselves out as, and are accepted by the public as possessing special knowledge and skills in a widely recognised body of learning derived from research, education and training at a high level, and who are prepared to apply this knowledge and exercise these skills in the interest of others.
>
> It is inherent in the definition of a Profession that a code of ethics governs the activities of each Profession. Such codes require behaviour and practice beyond the personal moral obligations of an individual. They define and demand high standards of behaviour in respect to the services provided to the public and in dealing with professional colleagues. Further, these codes are enforced by the Profession and are acknowledged and accepted by the community.

In the UK, various professions make clear the centrality of the 'ethical' to the nature of the profession. For example, in its Code of Ethics,[2] the British Association of Social Workers asserts that:

> Ethical awareness is fundamental to the professional practice of social workers. Their ability and commitment to act ethically is an essential aspect of the quality of the service offered to those who engage with social workers. Respect for human rights and a commitment to promoting social justice are at the core of social work practice throughout the world.

The Law Society of England and Wales[3] makes clear that

- The commitment to behaving ethically is at the heart of what it means to be a solicitor.
- Ethics is based on the principles of:
  - serving the interests of consumers of legal services
  - acting in the interests of justice acting with integrity and honesty according to widely recognised moral principles
- Ethics will help you respond in the right way to any moral dilemmas you might face at work.

Many more codes of conduct from other professions that similarly locate ethical conduct as fundamental to the profession could be cited.

However, despite these reasonably well established and understood definitions, how best the ethical should be formulated conceptually and can be implemented practically remains both disputed and challenging. Clearly, ideas about what constitutes the 'good' professional transcend core technical abilities and encompass notions of judgement, wisdom and care. Questions remain about the extent to which particular cultures, discourses and practices can put pressure on how professionals, particularly those working in the public sector, can act with (or indeed without) ethics and integrity (see, for example, Furlong et al. 2017). Indeed, various studies evidence the impact (whether positive or negative) of workplace conditions on professionals' ability to exhibit ethical conduct (see, for example, Oakley and Cocking, 2001; RPS, 2011; OfSTED, 2019a; Worth and Van Den Brande, 2019).

Discussions about the meaning and nature of ethical professional conduct and the effect of cultures, discourses and workplace practices typically concentrate around two particular considerations. The first is the impact, widely cited and critiqued in current literature on ethics and the professions, of the increased forms of managerialism and instrumentalism that are viewed as acting to detract from the ethical and societal role of professionals. According to critics, the turn to managerialism across and within the professions has led not to a renewed form of professionalism but to processes of de- and re-professionalisation through which the goals of general accountability (to service-users and to government) and efficiency have actively worked against professional autonomy and judgement (Holbeche and Springett, 2004; Carr, 2011; Dixon-Woods, Yeung and Bosk, 2011). The second consideration is the extent to which professions, such as nursing, teaching and social work, have come under increased public scrutiny and accountability in the wake of various 'scandals' (Seijts, Crossan and Carleton, 2017; Arthur et al., 2019a). Over the last 25 years in England, for example, high profile cases including the murder of Stephen Lawrence and resulting Stephen Lawrence Inquiry and Macpherson Report, the murder of Victoria Climbié, the death of Peter Connelly (also known as Baby P), the Mid Staffordshire hospital crisis, and the Rotherham Child Sexual Exploitation scandal have all raised serious questions about what were significant failures in professionals' ethical judgement and conduct.

In the context of managerialism, accountability, efficiency, public scrutiny and increased workplace pressures, professions and professionals need to (re)envisage the ethical nature of their work.

This (re)envisaging by necessity includes paying attention to what a profession aspires to be, what constitutes professional practice – whether generally or specifically for that profession – and how external factors shape the standing and work of professions today. In the next section, we start to examine these questions through a focus on a virtue-based approach to professional ethics. In doing so, we introduce key work in the field, particularly that which makes reference to the concept of professional *phronesis*.

A virtue-based approach to professional ethics

The last few decades have witnessed a groundswell of interest in virtue-based approaches to professional ethics. Though not the only variant of a virtue-ethical approach, the vast majority of this interest has drawn on Aristotelian roots, and this concerted interest in Aristotelian/neo-Aristotelian virtue has been applied across of a range of professional contexts, including accountancy (West, 2017), medicine (Pellegrino and Thomasma, 1993; Kotzee, Paton and Conroy, 2016), nursing (McKie et al., 2012), social work (Adam, 2009) and youth work (Bessant, 2009). In particular, two Aristotelian ideas have provoked significant interest among those concerned with professional ethics. The first is the idea that virtues represent 'contextually appropriate traits... such as honesty, compassion and perseverance' that contra rules 'become habitually ingrained through deliberate and repetitive practice, predisposing practitioners to behave based on ethically sound habits' (Arthur et al., 2019b: 2). The second idea – the main focus of this section – is the concept of *phronesis*, or practical wisdom (Pellegrino and Thomasma, 1993; Kinsella and Pitman, 2012; McKie et al., 2012). It is important to note, here, that while often cited, *phronesis* is not understood *uniformly* throughout the literature on professions (for a useful overview of *phronesis* in medical practice, see Kotzee, Paton and Conroy, 2016). Indeed, examining work on *phronesis* in professional medical ethics, Kristjánsson (2015b: 299) highlights the 'considerable lack of clarity in the current discursive field on *phronesis*'

In line with its neo-Aristotelian philosophy, the Jubilee Centre advocates the following model of the **Building Blocks of Professional Practice** (see Figure 1.1).

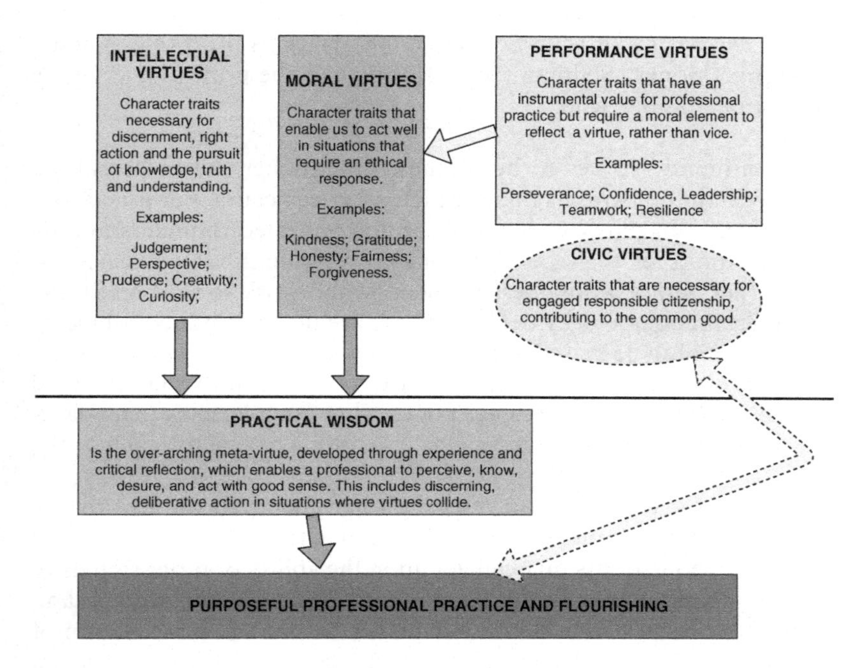

Figure 1.1 The Building Blocks of Professional Practice. The Jubilee Centre's *A Framework for Character Education in Schools* (2017) adapted to a professional domain. The model depicts the four domains of virtue and their conceptual relationship with practical wisdom and the purposeful professional practice.

In Figure 1.1, *phronesis* – or practical wisdom – is defined as 'the over-arching meta-virtue, developed through experience and critical reflection, which enables a professional to perceive, know, desire and act with good sense. This includes discerning, deliberative action in situations where virtues collide'. In other words, professionals need a certain form of practical wisdom, or *phronesis*, which can be defined in the following way:

> To practice with *phronesis* is to act with care, diligence and open-mindedness. To practice without *phronesis* would mean acting carelessly, indecisively, and with a degree of negligence to the surrounding circumstances or possible consequences.
>
> (Arthur et al., 2019b: 5)

For some authors, it is possible and useful to identify a form of professional *phronesis* – or what Sellman (2009: 1) terms the 'professionally wise practitioner'. Sellman (2012: 116) defines the professionally wise practitioner as one who:

> continually strives to be the best practitioner she or he can be given the constraints under which practice occurs. For practitioners, this endeavor includes but is not restricted to understanding the limits of their own personal professional competencies together with a willingness to identify and work toward rectifying relevant competency deficits. These are demanding requirements that imply a deep understanding of the turbulent and dynamic nature of practice, a recognition of the value of some form of critical self-reflection, and a resolve not to allow complacency to jeopardise future practice.

As Sellman makes clear, an important consideration for any virtue-based account of professional conduct and activity is to recognise the situational constraints that can act upon the ability of professionals to conduct themselves ethically. As Pitman (2012: 131) has argued, and as we have suggested above, the managerialism and marketisation of public professions such as teaching, health care professions and social work have created a 'hostile ground for growing phronesis' (see also Dixon-Woods, Yeung and Bosk, 2011. To neglect these factors is inherently problematic, as Kinsella and Pitman (2012: 8) remind us:

> as the mechanisms of professionalization have been put in place, so too have the levels of prescription increased, thereby circumscribing the capacity of members to act autonomously in situations that demand the exercise of judgement. The 'danger' of calling for phronesis and holding practitioners accountable for practical wisdom in contexts that may not support it, and that actively mitigate against it, is that practitioners may face a double bind, where they are blamed for a failure of agency at the personal level, when the issues may well be structural and systemic.

It is under such circumstances that moral and intellectual virtues – including the meta-virtue of *phronesis* – play a crucial role, enabling professionals to discern and deliberate about the correct course of actions given the *salient features at play*. Indeed, initial findings from a meta-analysis of professional virtues undertaken by the Jubilee Centre (Arthur et al., 2019a: 5) indicate that the '*phronetic* professional is one that is posited to endorse both moral and intellectual virtues in conjunction with one another'. These initial findings suggest 'the importance of developing a *phronetic* character profile for the enhancement of perceived professional purpose. That is, one that encompasses a value for both moral and intellectual virtue simultaneously as opposed to in isolation of one another'. Importantly, moral virtues may be crucial for developing a sense of purpose that extends beyond the self to the community in which one works, but 'it is only when a moral compass is synergised with a valuation of the intellectual virtues, that professionals are likely to experience the greatest possible sense of professional purpose' (Arthur et al., 2019a: 16). In other words, moral and intellectual values work together to guide right action and a deeper sense of professional worth.

Codes of conduct and the limitations of rule

A core feature of professional occupations, then, is the ability to handle the ethical dilemmas and challenges faced within the workplace. Given its complexity and the challenges involved in delineating an ethically appropriate course of action, professional work is such that the professional cannot simply follow given guidelines or codes – particularly when ethical requirements conflict (for example, when loyalty conflicts with honesty). So too, and given the complex nature and scope of professional activity, the professional must draw on a range of salient information – theories, practices, prevalent codes, relationships involved, potential outcomes – to discern the right course of action for the right reasons. In certain circumstances, the complexity and challenges of their occupation may place professionals in situations where their actions may be both morally right and yet run counter to the requirements set out by government and related agencies. As Carr (1999: 35) contends, 'responsible professional decisions must depend ultimately on the quality of *personal* deliberation and reflection'.

This is not to suggest, however, that the sort of practical wisdom needed for professional *phronesis* can be completely separated from the principles and rules that often characterise professional codes of conduct (Pellegrino and Thomasma, 1993). Having a clearly stated set of principles and rules brings a number of benefits in terms of educating new entrants to the profession, guiding professional conduct and providing those external to the profession (patients, clients, parents, pupils, etc.) with some understanding of what can be expected of the profession concerned. However, rules and codes of conduct can only help the professional so far and are insufficient for true ethical practice if they are not accompanied, interpreted and balanced by intellectual and moral character. In simple terms, where codes of conduct are too rigid, cultures of conformity can undermine professional autonomy and judgement; where codes of conduct are overly ambiguous, they offer professionals little by way of structure and guidance to inform their deliberations and choices.

American psychologist Barry Schwartz has spoken about the ways in which the dominance of external controls, such as rules and incentives, can actively *undermine* wisdom and judgement. According to Schwartz (2009):

> rules and incentives may make things better in the short run, but they create a downward spiral that makes them worse in the long run. Moral skill is chipped away by an over-reliance on rules that deprives us of the opportunity to improvise and learn from our improvisations. And moral will is undermined by an incessant appeal to incentives that destroy our desire to do the right thing. And without intending it, by appealing to rules and incentives, we are engaging in a war on wisdom.

Importantly for the focus of this book, Schwartz (2011) has also argued that the dominance of rules and incentives does not only limit professional wisdom but also serves to undermine professional motivation. He argues that:

> the problem with relying on rules and incentives is that they demoralize professional activity, and they demoralize professional activity in two senses. First, they demoralize the people who are engaged in the activity. And second, they demoralize the activity itself. The very practice is demoralized, and the practitioners are demoralized. It creates people – when you manipulate incentives to get people to do the right thing – it creates people who are addicted to incentives. That is to say, it creates people who only do things for incentives.

The *phronetic* professional, then, is not guided solely by duty to codes external to their own intellect and morals or by externally driven incentives, but rather conceives and applies their professional responsibilities by using their professional wisdom. This includes understanding codes of conduct but not conceiving these as the sole arbiter when dilemmas arise. As the author C. S. Lewis (1985: 100; cited in Bohlin, 2005: 20) eloquently wrote in his *Letters to Children*:

> A prefect man would never act from a sense of duty; he'd always want the right thing more than the wrong one. Duty is only a substitute for love (of God and other people), like a crutch, which is the substitute for a leg. Most of us need the crutch at times; but of course its idiotic to use the crutch when our legs (our own loves, tastes, habits etc) can do the journey on their own.

Lewis' words remind us that sound professional conduct has an internal motivation and meaning – that is, it must come from the heart. It is for precisely this reason that many, if not all, professions are understood as vocations rather than simply occupations.

Focusing on the sorts of capacities frequently associated with professional *phronesis*, which include sensitivity, discernment, deliberation and reflection, signifies that the codification of professional conduct into a set of rules cannot be disentangled from the critical judgement of the professional. Indeed, the critical judgement of the professional is crucial if those rules are to be applied in practice, and in a way that juggles the demands of the specific situation at hand (including where stated rules may be in conflict). Whether one subscribes to an Aristotelian notion of *phronesis* that separates ethical from technical practice or from a MacIntyrean approach that understands technical practice to have an ethical dimension, it remains that the ethical is core to professional practice (Cooke and Carr, 2014; Kristjánsson, 2015b; Kotzee, Paton and Conroy, 2016).

Conclusion

In this chapter we have surveyed existing literature on the ethical dimensions of professions. As we have intimated in the chapter, it is not a question of *whether* professions such as medicine, law, nursing, social work, and teaching involve an ethical dimension but rather how this dimension is and should be conceived and enacted by these professions. While general approaches to professional ethics act as a significant starting point in responding to these latter questions, the nature, demands and realities of professional ethics are necessarily moderated by the particular profession at hand. In other words, while we might approach the general ethical dimensions of professions from a given framework (in the case of the Jubilee Centre, a broadly neo-Aristotelian one), it is also necessary to appreciate that the precise ethical demands that act upon doctors, nurses, lawyers, teachers and so on are likely to be framed and expressed in ways particular to those individuals professions. With this in mind, the focus of the next chapter more specifically on ethics and the teaching profession.

Notes

1 www.professions.com.au/about-us/what-is-a-professional.
2 www.basw.co.uk/about-basw/code-ethics.
3 www.lawsociety.org.uk/support-services/ethics/.

2 Ethics and the teaching profession

Introduction

Historically, education has aimed at moral formation, with teaching understood as a markedly moral relationship between the teacher and the child. While statements about the moral basis of teaching remain common, if not universal, it is also fair to say that over the last few decades, education and schooling have taken a more instrumental term, and today many teachers would understand their role as primarily being concerned with preparing students for academic success and for their working lives after school. This instrumental turn in how education and teaching is framed and practiced has been brought about by a series of reforms to education, schooling systems, teacher preparation, and the curriculum that have prioritised a conception of the teacher as someone who possesses strong subject knowledge and is adept at the technical aspects of teaching. But while both subject knowledge and proficiency in teaching subjects are important, ignoring the moral dimensions of teaching leads to a partial and impoverished idea of what it means to be a *good* teacher.

This chapter is concerned with the ethical requirements of teaching as a profession and how ethics are central to being a good teacher. Understanding teaching as an essentially ethical profession, and education as a moral enterprise (Carr, 1993), the chapter examines the moral dimensions of teaching and the role of the teacher. Teachers are a central means through which the values and commitments of schools, communities, and wider society are cultivated within the young. As stated above, the claims (1) that teaching is a moral endeavour and (2) that it is precisely because of this that teaching should be regarded as a *profession* are now fairly consistent in the educational literature (Tom, 1984; Strike and Soltis, 1985; Carr, 1991; 1999, 2000, 2007; Hansen, 2001; Arthur, 2003; Cooke and Carr, 2014). Concerns remain, however, about the extent to which the moral dimensions of teaching are appreciated in practice (Arthur, 2003; Maxwell and Schwimmer, 2016). In the UK, few empirical studies have been conducted that have explored how teachers conceive and implement their moral role. As such, this chapter and the arguments within it pave the way for the empirical data presented and analysed in subsequent chapters.

The teaching profession

A number of studies across a range of contexts suggest a relatively substantial and certainly persistent interest in the professional ethics of teachers (Goodfellow, 2003; Shapira-Lishchinsky, 2009; Boon, 2011; Hendrikx, 2019; Ulvik, Smith and Helleve, 2017). Writing in the 1990s, for example, John Wilson (1993: 113) contended that:

> Moral qualities are directly relevant to any kind of classroom practice: care for the pupils, enthusiasm for the subject, conscientiousness, determination, willingness to cooperate with colleagues and a host of others. Nobody, at least on reflection, really believes that effective teaching – let alone effective education – can be reduced to a set of skills; it requires certain dispositions of character. The attempt to avoid the question of what these dispositions are by employing pseudo-practical terms like 'competence' or 'professional' must fail.

Following suit, the vast majority of work on teacher ethics over the last 30 years identifies the ethical dimension of teaching as a cornerstone for understanding teaching as a specifically *professional* activity (Campbell, 2008). As Elliott (1989: 9) suggests:

> When teachers are viewed as practitioners of an ethic then they may be described appropriately as members of a *profession*. But when their activity is viewed as a kind of technology then their status may simply be reduced to that of the technician.

Often, the analyses offered in studies of teacher professionalism focus on the value of developing ethical codes of conduct as a precondition for professionalism (Campbell, 2000; Schwimmer and Maxwell, 2017), and many countries now have codes of ethical conducts for teachers. Similarly to other professions, such codes seek to encapsulate a set of ethical norms or standards to which members of that profession commit, and which they uphold within their professional lives. In this way, codes of professional conduct – such as those found in the Teachers' Standards in England to which we return below – act as an external guide for ethical practice. Ethical codes of conducts or standards are also seen to play a crucial role in preparing new members of the teaching profession, with student and beginning teachers being educated about their provisions and implications (Campbell, 2011; Maxwell and Schwimmer, 2016).

As was suggested in the previous chapter with regard to professions more generally, while codes of conduct act as important markers of what ethically is expected of the teaching profession, and are particularly important in providing clarity for external audiences such as parents, in and of themselves these codes do not necessarily solidify the core attributes nor the depth of moral commitment required of a good teacher. This is for a number of reasons. First and foremost, codes remain external to the individual, focusing that is on what the teacher *should do* rather than the sort of person the teacher *should be.* In focusing predominantly on cognitive matters (knowing what to do and why), codes frequently say little about moral motivations and moral emotions, both of which form core components of morality. As such, when codes are presented as a set of competencies or standards they do not (indeed cannot) capture the complex and nuanced entirety of human abilities, making meaningful assessment of these competencies or standards challenging to say the least. Second, and connected, codes run the risk of drawing too sharply the distinction between professional and personal ethics (Carr, 1999; Arthur, Davison and Lewis, 2005). As Carr (1999) has argued, so far as teaching is concerned, it does seem to matter whether a teacher is a particular (good) sort of person outside of their particular technical functions as a teacher (educating subject knowledge, maintaining an orderly learning environment etc.). Third, ethical codes of conduct can limit the professional judgement and autonomy of the teacher, particularly where those codes are 'regulatory' in nature, providing a static and detached way of conceiving ethical principles in a way dissociated from the reality of teachers' lives and experiences (Schwimmer and Maxwell, 2017: 142; see also, Cigman, 2000). Indeed, Ladd (1998: 211) critiques codes of ethics on the following basis:

> Ethical principles can be established only as a result of deliberation and argumentation. These principles are not the kind of thing that can be settled by fiat, by agreement or by authority. To assume that they can be is to confuse ethics with law-making, rule-making, policy-making and other kinds of decision-making.

> It follows that, ethical principles, as such cannot be established by associations, organisations, or by consensus of their members.

While not wishing to discount the utility of codes of conduct completely (see Banks, 2003, for a conditional justification of codes of conducts in the profession), in line with the wider work and core commitments of the *Jubilee Centre for Character and Virtues*, we suggest that understanding teaching as a profession is better approached from a virtue-based perspective that concentrates not on codes of conduct but on character. Focusing on the character of the good teacher helps to move on from codes of conduct or standards in order to think more carefully about how ethical conduct actually operates in practice; how, that is, the general pronouncements and aspiration of the code are interpreted and enacted by teachers. As set out in *A Framework for Character Education in Schools*, and as explained in previous chapters, the Jubilee Centre for Character and Virtues adopts a neo-Aristotelian approach to character and character education. Virtues are conceived as 'those character traits that enable human beings to respond appropriately to situations in any area of experience' (Jubilee Centre, 2017). The Framework states the moral role of the teachers as character educators in the following terms:

> In order to be a good teacher, one needs to be or become a certain kind of person: a person of good character who also exemplifies commitment to the value of what they teach. The character and integrity of the teacher is more fundamental than personality or personal style in class, and it is no less important than mastery of subject content and techniques of instruction... Good teaching is underpinned by an ethos and language that enables a public discussion of character within the school community so that good character permeates all subject teaching and learning.
>
> (2017: 9–10)

A core element of the virtue ethical approach to education and teaching adopted by the Centre is that if they are to fulfil their moral role, teachers – as with all moral agents – need to develop a form of practical wisdom (or *phronesis*). In general terms, practical wisdom is 'the integrative virtue, developed through experience and critical reflection, which enables us to perceive, know, desire and act with good sense. This includes discerning, deliberative action in situations where virtues collide' (Jubilee Centre, 2017: 5). It is through practical wisdom that people are able to discern the salient features of a given situation, to deliberate about what these features entail and the various options available to them, and to make a sound judgement about what course of action should be taken. Taking the idea of practical wisdom into the sphere of teaching, we would argue that what is involved is *professional practical wisdom* (Schwartz, 2014). Through professional practical wisdom, teachers are sensitive to their own moral character, to the moral requirements of their wider profession and to the morally salient features of the situations they face *as teachers*. Professional practical wisdom enables teachers to judge and enact the right response, for the right reasons and at the right times. Importantly, this professional practical wisdom can be differentiated from the more widespread concept of the 'reflective practitioner'. Higgins (2001: 93) usefully explains the difference between the reflective practitioner and *phronesis* in the following terms: 'If the unreflective practitioner lacks *phronesis*, then unreflectiveness is not merely inflexibility but a kind of moral blindness. Unable to see what the new demands of us, we fall prey to various forms of repetition'.

The recent resurgence of interest in character education provides an important opportunity to reignite the commitment to understanding teaching as an ethical profession. In the last six years in England, several Secretaries of State for Education have affirmed the importance of character education (Morgan, 2014; Hinds, 2019). Although the use of the term 'character' is sometimes lacking in precision in its usage in political debates and is consistently connected to traits such as resilience and determination, there is evidence of a more positive moral commitment as part of the government's commitment. Speaking early in 2019, then Secretary of State for Education, Damian Hinds (2019), asserted the importance of cultivating children's character and that 'character must be grounded in virtues, in strong values'. OfSTED's new Education Inspection Framework (2019b) includes a new focus on students' personal development, including the development of their character, their active citizenship and their understanding and appreciation of diversity. These aspects clearly speak to the ethical facets of teachers' work, including how they develop the character of their pupils.

Of course, teacher professionalism occurs and is enacted within particular contexts. While traditionally in the United Kingdom – and indeed elsewhere – education has been viewed as incorporating concern for the moral, ethical and social development of the child (Arthur, 2003), over the last three decades or more the trajectory of much educational policy has been to reduce the moral role of both the teacher and education more generally. A range of policy moves have brought about a more instrumental approach to education, which in turn have impacted negatively on levels of teacher autonomy and have fundamentally re-shaped the public role of teachers/teaching. These policy moves include: the marketisation of education through competition, choice and testing; the focus on measurable "outputs" and "outcomes", particularly through the use of standardised testing; the narrowing of the curriculum towards a more limited range of subject disciplines; the de-contextualisation of education policies and initiatives through increased "policy-borrowing" and a culture of "what works"; the introduction of new managerialism; and, changes to the nature and requirements of pre-service teacher education to focus on more practical, instrumental elements of teaching (behaviour management, lesson planning, and assessment, for example; for an overview of this crucial shift in teacher education in the 1990s and early 2000s, see Arthur, Davison and Lewis, 2005).

Furthermore, concerns over standards and disciplinary subject knowledge have led to a succession of initiatives that have increased standardisation, formal accountability and control of teachers' work (Ball, 2003). The cumulative effects of these policy trends have been to narrow the focus, content and practice of education, moving schools and teachers away from their traditional role in cultivating the character of the child. There is also evidence that, in some schools, the impacts of neoliberal and neoconservative policies have led to instrumental and narrow forms of moral education (Dishon and Goodman, 2017), as well as giving rise to a gap between how teachers understand the profession normatively and how they act in practice (Hendrikx, 2019). Such concerns are now relatively longstanding. Writing at the turn of the new millennium, Tomlinson (2001: 36) reflected that teachers had become 'a technical workforce to be managed and controlled rather than a profession to be respected'.

These trends have continued apace and seem to be having some concerning effects. In 2019, the UK's Health and Safety Executive reported that teaching staff and educational professionals reported high levels of work-related stress, depression and anxiety compared to other occupational groups.[1] In a recent report on teacher well-being at work in England, the Office for Standards in Education, Children's Services and Skills (OfSTED, 2019a) reported that:

> Teachers in both schools and further education and skills (FES) providers love their profession, overwhelmingly enjoy teaching, are generally very positive about their workplace and colleagues, enjoy building relationships with pupils and seeing them flourish. However, these positive elements of well-being at work are counterbalanced by negative elements that lead to poor occupational

> well-being for many teachers… teachers are suffering from high workloads, lack of work-life balance, a perceived lack of resources and, in some cases, a perceived lack of support from senior managers… They sometimes feel the profession does not receive the respect it deserves.

Statements such as this remind us that the challenges of being a good teacher are not just internal to individual teachers (their own character, values, etc.) or to individual schools (school ethos, culture, etc.), and that externally driven factors (government policy, public perceptions, etc.) also place pressure on the work of teachers as well as on teaching's status as a profession.

Notably, however, and as intimated above, while education policy in England has been dominated by instrumental concerns, it would be wrong to suggest that there has been *no* policy interest in the moral dimensions of teaching. Policy initiatives within various jurisdictions over the last two decades, in different ways and to different extents, have touched upon the moral role of the teacher. If we consider English education policy, these include policies for citizenship education, community cohesion, SMSC (social, moral, spiritual and cultural development), religious education, in addition to character education itself. Furthermore, the current Teachers' Standards[2] published by the Department for Education in 2011 comprise two parts: Teaching, and Personal and Professional Conduct. The provisions for Personal and Professional Conduct include that teachers must 'maintain high standards of ethics and behaviour, within and outside school, including by treating pupils with dignity, building relationships rooted in mutual respect and at all times observing proper boundaries appropriate to a teacher's professional position' (DfE, 2011: 14). By paying explicit attention to Personal and Professional Conduct, the standards draw attention to the ethical relationships involved in teaching, though it remains another matter how the standards are actually understood and implemented by schools, teachers and providers of initial teacher education.

Teachers of character

To this point we have argued that though teaching comprises a number of different attributes, dispositions and skills, it is an essentially moral endeavour. The 'good' teacher is someone who understands that strong subject knowledge and mastery of the craft of teaching are not all that teaching requires and who appreciate their moral role. Recognising that the moral nature of teaching is complex and brings many challenges, good teachers conduct themselves with virtues such as honesty, integrity, compassion and civility, seeking in turn to foster these virtues in their students (Gardner, Csikszentmihalyi and Damon, 2001; Campbell, 2011, 2013; Sockett, 2012; Damon and Colby, 2014). Indeed, part of the complexity of examining and understanding the ethics of the teacher is that teachers are expected both to be of good moral standing *and* to develop the moral standing of their students, and there are strong reasons for suggesting that the latter depends in important ways on the former (Carr, 1991, 2007; Arthur, Davison and Lewis, 2005; Osguthorpe, 2008).

When teachers ask students to engage with particular ideas and texts, when teachers seek to develop certain behaviours and ways of thinking in their students and when teachers promote positive values and relationships within their classrooms and schools, they are – whether explicitly or implicitly – undertaking a moral role. Furthermore, teachers act, intentionally or otherwise, as moral role models, providing an example to their students through their approach and actions. Fenstermacher (1990: 133; see also De Ruyter and Kole, 2010) summarises the various moral contours of teaching well:

> What makes teaching a moral endeavour is that it is, quite centrally, human action undertaken in regard to other human beings. Thus, matters of what is fair, right, just, and virtuous are always present. Whenever a teacher asks a student to share something with another student, decides between combatants in a schoolyard dispute, sets procedures for who will go first, second, third, and so on, or discusses the welfare of a student with another teacher, moral considerations are present. The teacher's conduct, at all times and in all ways, is a moral matter. For that reason alone, teaching is a profoundly moral activity… the teacher is a role model for the students, such that the particular and concrete meaning of such traits as honesty, fair play, consideration of others, tolerance, and sharing are "picked up", as it were, by observing, imitating, and discussing what teachers do in classrooms.

Previous research that has examined the moral dimensions of teaching evidences that teachers are aware of their moral role (Boon, 2011; Campbell, 2011; Arthur and Revell, 2012; Sanger and Osguthorpe, 2011, 2013; Maxwell and Schwimmer, 2016), that they seek to make a positive difference to their students (Osguthorpe and Sanger, 2013), but that teachers often find the content and boundaries of their moral role difficult to grasp and enact (Cummings, Harlow and Maddux, 2007; Mahoney, 2009).

Some researchers are concerned that the marginalisation of the moral dimensions of teaching has led to a situation in which teachers – and indeed teacher educators – operate without a clear and meaningful 'moral language' (Sockett and LePage, 2002; Campbell, 2008; Sanger and Osguthorpe, 2011), while others have pointed to the negative impact of instrumentalised cultures of efficiency and accountability on teachers' own well-being and motivations (Kidger et al. 2016).

Of relevance, too, are theoretical and empirically substantiated concerns that teachers often adopt an overly "neutral" or narrow approach to moral issues in the classroom on the basis that they are either unsure or insecure about adopting a particular moral position (Arthur, 2003; Walsh and Casinader, 2019). When teachers respond in these ways, morals are either neglected or are limited to an examination of values held by students or by the class. Being a moral educator is a challenging task but is one from which teachers cannot, and should not, be excused. It should also be noted that amid wide concerns about the perceived value of the teaching profession and attrition rates, research suggests that it is often the ethical aspects of teaching which motivate new entrants to the profession and keep teachers committed to their work (Goodfellow, 2003; Belogolovsky and Somech, 2010; Peterson and Bentley, 2017; Perryman and Calvert, 2019).

Of course, moral formation cannot ever be the task of schools and teachers alone. Families and parents remain the primary moral educator of children, and peer-groups, media, faith traditions, and community associations also play a part. Good teachers enact their ethical responsibilities in union with others, and part of the ethical understanding teachers require is to appreciate what these relationships require of them and how wider social connections shape the moral dimensions of their work.

Before concluding, we should also raise briefly two further, important reflections. The first is that while research on the moral role of teachers has been undertaken in the United States over a number of years (Colby and Damon, 1992; Damon and Colby, 2014), before the research conducted by the Jubilee Centre for Character and Virtues, very few empirical studies exploring how teachers understood and approached the moral dimensions of their work had been undertaken in the United Kingdom. One reason for this lack of empirical work is that developing and implementing empirical measurements of the moral dimensions of teaching is not an easy task. Previous empirical research from elsewhere in the area of teaching from an ethical perspective has typically used three broad methods: observation (Fallona, 2000; Buzzelli and Johnston, 2001), reflection and interviews

(Elbaz, 1992; Sockett and LePage, 2002; Husu and Tirri, 2003, 2007; Mahoney, 2009), and ethical dilemmas or critical incidents (Strike and Soltis, 2009). The second reflection is that while ethical codes of conduct may be problematic because they are too minimal in their depiction of the morality of teaching (Schwimmer and Maxwell, 2017), there are also important boundaries and limits to the moral role of teachers. Most pertinently, and as Campbell (2008: 612) argues, 'ethical teachers should be moral agents and moral models, not moralistic activists'. Campbell's point here acts as an important reminder that good teachers use their judgement and professional wisdom to act within appropriate moral frameworks, including deliberating within themselves and with others about the ethical boundaries of their work.

Conclusion

Recognising that teaching is a relational activity between humans, and that teachers operate within certain conditions, laws and circumstances, we would argue that good teachers care about their students, recognising and cultivating what is good in them and being positively concerned with who they are and might become. A fundamental sphere of this relationship of care is students' moral development and well-being. Good teachers take a supportive, proactive and reflective stance towards their own character and their students' character development, not least when students are facing particular challenges in their lives. The aim here is not to produce uncritical conformity and to take away from the autonomy of students (that would be indoctrination) but is rather to induct children into the norms of their schools and communities. This moral induction includes teaching students to adopt a critical and deliberative standpoint, and supports them in examining the real challenges that morality poses. In other words, good teachers forge a path that avoids locating morality as a solely a personal, subjective concern while at the same time enabling sufficient scope for contested moral ideas to be examined and discussed. An important way that good teachers forge such a path, one that is based on sound preparation and a supportive wider environment, is through their own modelling of character traits such as honesty, integrity, humility, and compassion.

Notes

1 www.hse.gov.uk/statistics/causdis/stress.pdf
2 https://assets.publishing.service.gov.uk/government/uploads/system/uploads/attachment_data/file/665520/Teachers_Standards.pdf

3 Teachers and character education

Motivations, roles and preparation

Introduction

In this chapter we present, analyse and discuss empirical data drawn from Jubilee Centre projects – *The Good Teacher* (Arthur et al., 2015a), *Teacher Education* (Arthur et al., 2018a) and *Schools of Virtue* (Arthur et al., 2017) – which have examined how teachers at various stages of their career – Student Teachers, Newly Qualified Teachers and Experienced Teachers – conceive character in relation to their roles as a teacher and to teaching as a profession more widely. The chapter consists of three sections. In the first, data is presented which found that general notions of character and 'making a difference to the lives of children' form an important part of what motivates entrants to the profession. In the second section, focus turns to how respondents conceive their role in developing young people's character. Across the main three studies on which this book is based, teachers at various career stages have reported that they do view themselves as having an important role to play in pupils' character development. Yet, and as is analysed in the section, evidence from these projects suggests that as teachers progress in their careers, this role in character development becomes focused increasingly on performance virtues (such as perseverance and determination). The third section centres on preparing teachers for their role in character development. In this section respondents' perspectives on the extent to and ways in which their teacher education and professional development experiences had prepared them for developing pupils' character are examined.

Motivation to teach

In the preceding chapters, the nature of professionalism was explored generally (Chapter 1) and with specific regard to teaching (Chapter 2).

In these chapters, we argued both that ethics was a core component of what constitutes a profession and that the ethical domain of professionalism was best conceived and approached from a virtue ethics perspective. In these chapters we also suggested that the ethical nature of professional work played an important role in motivating people to join a profession in the first place. In short, teachers are motivated to join the profession largely by the goal of making a difference to pupils' lives.

Questions about why people choose to join the teaching profession and about what motivates them to stay or leave the profession have received significant attention in England over the last decade or so in the face of a teacher recruitment crisis (Coughlan, 2018; Foster, 2019; See and Gorard, 2019). In The Jubilee Centre's *The Good Teacher* project, participants were asked (through an open-ended question in the questionnaire and in interviews) about their motivations to join the teaching profession. Responses were analysed as falling into three broad themes, each drawn from recent research on motivation to teach (Ewing and Manuel, 2005; Manuel and Hughes, 2006; Thomson, Turner and Nietfield, 2012). These were: altruism (to benefit others), intrinsic worth (because it matters to the self) and extrinsic benefits (external conditions or rewards) (Arthur et al., 2015).

In the responses, the majority of participants from across all career stages combined altruistic with intrinsic values when explaining their motivation to teach as illustrated by the following participant (a newly qualified teacher):

> I think it is a very noble profession, very rewarding, a fun job, not boring and I can continue to work with my languages and young people as well. *NQT*

The second most reported combination, across all career stages, was the combination of intrinsic and extrinsic themes. This response from an Experienced Teacher was indicative:

> There was a mixture of it seeming to be a natural and normal thing to do from growing up, a real genuine sense of vocation and particularly the teaching of my subject being something I wanted to do; but also the fact that it was a viable, financially rewarding career. *Exp Tchr*

Across the sample, analysis showed that respondents from all career stages reported their motivation to teach as resting largely on intrinsic factors, whether these intrinsic factors operated alone or in combination with altruistic or extrinsic themes. Those who referred to the intrinsic motivation of 'enjoying teaching' often did so in relation to their previous work experience with children (e.g. coaching a football team, or volunteering with young people) (Arthur et al., 2017).

Analysis of the responses also evidenced that altruistic considerations emerged when teachers from all career stages talked about wanting to 'make a difference' and/or about wanting to 'impart wisdom or knowledge':

> To make a difference, because I think I can contribute something and I feel I could add something to the value of, I don't know, on the bigger scheme of things, value of humanity. *Exp Tchr*

> I chose it because I've always had a passion for my subject primarily and it's not only a career that will enable me to keep learning, but also to share that knowledge with young people. *NQT*

> To do a worthwhile job where I could share my love of learning and make a useful contribution to society. *Exp Tchr*

It is worth noting, too, that no participants cited extrinsic factors as their *sole* motivation to teach. In other words, extrinsic factors were always cited in combination with either (or both) altruistic and intrinsic factors.

Additional analysis of the open-ended responses in the questionnaire prompts some further reflections. For example, and as the following responses illustrate, for many respondents supporting the development of *pupils' character* was a core aspect of their motivation to become a teacher:

> I want to have a positive impact on the lives of others. I want to be a role model to future generations and encourage young pupils to make the right decisions. I want to inspire pupils to be the best they can, by setting high expectations and providing the opportunities for pupils to reach their full potential. I know I will find the profession highly rewarding. I enjoy working with young people and believe my character is suited to teaching. *Stdt Tchr*

> I love learning: coming to understand the world better and better. I think everyone should have the skills to investigate the world and develop themselves into maturity and adulthood, so that they can make the very best of themselves and have the most positive impact on their communities. Life is a context rich and complex experience, and we need to enable students to engage with it in a 'good' way.

> This concept of 'good' has for me some absolute features, based on respect for all, treating others as you would like them to treat you and taking a stewardship view of our responsibility toward the global community. This is, also, always tempered by a sceptical and inquisitive attitude to everything presented to them. *Stdt Tchr*

> I considered it to be a most rewarding career to have the opportunity to have a positive impact upon children's lives and life chances. *Exp Tchr*

> I think young people are awesome. They haven't had the spirit sucked out of them as much as adults… and I have always been critical of the way in which society brushes aside people because they do not have the right status or they are deemed of little value. I fundamentally believe that every person… has something wonderful to offer and is talented in some way… So it was my dream to train to be a teacher so I can get those kids at a young age and tell them they are worthy and show them how wonderful the world is and give them the confidence and skills to go out and make a difference and be good, happy and content. *NQT*

Respondents often combined a desire to inspire a love of learning (of subject or generally) in pupils with a concern for other aspects of character development. For example:

> Teaching is a rewarding profession as you get to see and help children to develop. This is both academically and in terms of their confidence and self-esteem. It is rewarding to see their improvement and the pride they feel and to know you have helped to achieve this. *NQT*

> A deep-seated belief that education affords opportunity and a belief that I can motivate, positively influence, guide and support young people at a formative and vulnerable time in their lives. A desire to share my love of learning, particularly with regard to the development of understanding in my subject area. *Exp Tchr*

> My reasons for entering the teaching profession is (sic) to encourage pupils to take responsibility for their lives and for themselves. I am to help pupils see their potential, despite however difficult their home life or background may be. I want to encourage pupils to respect themselves and work on their characters to become good young people, that respect and love one another and are of immense value to their communities. On another note, I love my

> subject (Science/Biology) and would also like to share the beauty of science and nature with the pupils I will get to teach. I feel teaching is one of the most important professions one can enter into in this day, and that those people need to be good, responsible role models as they take on the challenge of changing the lives of the pupils we interact with for the better. *NQT*

For another NQT, their own educational experiences shaped their motivation and commitment to their own teaching:

> I owe a great deal to my teachers, they contributed in no small part to where I am today. I feel very passionately that good teachers can change a person's life and unfortunately bad teachers can do the same. I believe I have the qualities and potential to become a good teacher and want the opportunity to have such a significant role; encouraging, inspiring and supporting children. I really enjoy being in schools and know that no matter how exhausted I feel or how challenging my day, I always leave feeling positive. Working with children opens up entirely new perspectives, which I find fascinating – I am constantly surprised, entertained and in awe of them, every day is a whirlwind of action that even makes all of the paperwork seem worthwhile. *NQT*

We end this section on teacher motivation with two further notes, both connected to the level of response to the open-ended question in the questionnaire regarding motivation for joining the teaching profession. The first is that the depth of response between participants varied in quite some length. Some respondents wrote extensive paragraphs to explain their motivation for joining the teaching profession, while others offered no more than a few words. This may, of course, be the result of no more than levels of engagement in the questionnaire or personal preference for brevity, but it was further notable that overall the length of response to the question of motivation was much higher for Student Teachers and NQTs than it was for Experienced Teachers. The second note is that responses from Experienced Teachers evidenced the sense in which the pressures of the job – accountability, time and so on – had detracted from their original motivation to enter the teaching profession.

Teachers of, and for, character

A further focus for analysis in the Centre's *The Good Teacher* project was how participants conceived their role in developing young people's character. When asked about developing character in young people, Experienced Teachers typically framed their responses in terms of moral and/or performance virtues. Indeed, and notably, the *main* emphasis across the data was on performance virtues such as perseverance and determination. When the importance of cultivating such performance virtues was discussed by Experienced Teachers, this was often connected to the need for young people to develop the attributes needed to 'cope' with and handle academic pressures, such as assessment. This said, there was consistent agreement from participants that it is the job of schools to build character and that this is an integral part of the work of schools. For example:

> You're not just there to cram in facts and information, you're there to make them into good people, good members of society. *Exp Tchr*

In line with the general tone of literature on character education, the Experienced Teachers in *The Good Teacher* study generally recognised that schools and teachers were a secondary source of moral development, and that the nature and extent of their work were influenced by other factors, including most notably the family/home:

> I don't think we should over-estimate the impact that we can have on some students. I think if you're looking for the school or college to be the be all and end all in developing a young person, that's not the case. *Exp Tchr*

Other links were also made by Experienced Teachers between their role/work and family influences on character development. For example, Experienced Teachers spoke about the time-demands and pressures placed on parents as well as the unrealistic expectations that some parents placed on teachers regarding the extent of their role with their children. An experienced secondary school teacher had the following to say:

> I could list on one hand the number of children out of 200 in Year 7 who actually get read a story or get to discuss something random at the dining table. We are the first port of call because parents are so busy. *Exp Tchr*

In talking about how they and their schools educate for character, Experienced Teachers spoke in terms of three, interconnected themes – all of which can be broadly correlated with what the Jubilee Centre refers to as 'character caught'. The first theme placed character education as integral to everything that happened in school. As one teacher, explained, character education is:

> Integral, you can't separate, you can't say 'we teach'... all the education goes on in the classroom anyway, about good behaviour and things like that, and what you should do. *Exp Tchr*

The second theme identified by the analysis was character learning through extra-curricular activities. A common reflection when Experienced Teachers spoke about these extra-curricular activities was that they aimed at instilling in pupils a sense of gratitude and an understanding of how fortunate they were in comparison to others:

> They go to old peoples' homes; they go to a special school and put on Christmas parties and stuff they wouldn't do. I think if we weren't doing that, the nature of the school would be lost. *Exp Tchr*

The third theme related to teachers acting as a role model to students, including how teachers sought to enact themselves the virtues they aimed to develop in their students (Arthur et al., 2017). Speaking about how teachers needed to conceptualise themselves, one teacher reflected:

> Maybe they need to just realise how much of a role model they are and how much that makes a difference to your classroom atmosphere ... how they can have such a positive influence if they are that positive role model. *Exp Tchr*

Data from the *Teacher Education* project evidences that from an early stage of their careers teachers conceive themselves as having an important role to play in pupils' moral education. Chart 3.1 shows that the vast majority of Student Teachers believed the development of a pupil's character was 'Important' or 'Very Important' in regard to their academic achievement. When compared, there were statistically significant differences between those from primary and secondary training settings in both initial survey and post survey responses. In the initial survey, 94.7% of student teachers from primary school settings reported that this was 'Very Important' or 'Important', compared to 90.2% of student teachers from secondary school settings. In the post survey, the figures were 94.7% for student teachers from primary school settings and 87.9% for student teachers from secondary school settings (Arthur et al., 2018a).

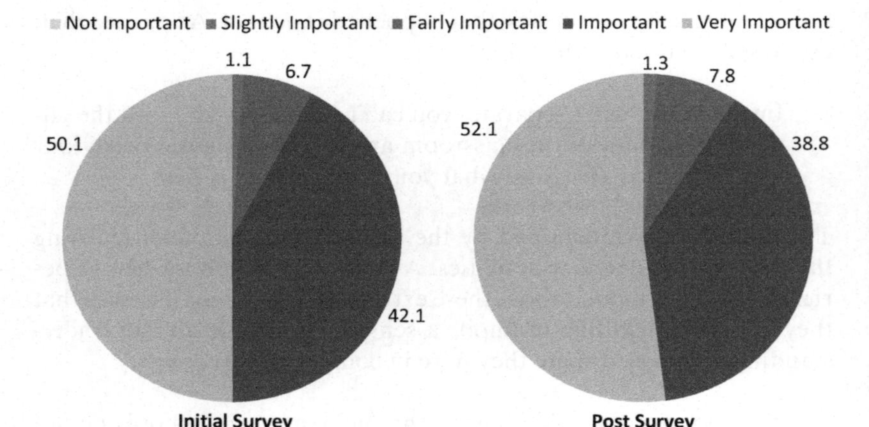

Chart 3.1 How Important Do You Think the Development of a Pupil's Character Is in Regards to their Academic Achievement?

The commitment of teachers to their work as moral educators also came through strongly in the three schools studied in the *Schools of Virtue* project. In each of the schools, teachers recognised that they are character 'educators', acting as 'role models' to pupils. Indeed, the effectiveness of the schools' vision for character education and the resulting implementation of those visions were understood to be dependent on staff 'buying into' the vision and conceiving themselves as character educators. Role modelling was reported by staff members as contributing to the consistency of the school's approach to character education. In all three schools, it was reinforced that staff should be aware that they are role models to pupils and should use a consistent virtue vocabulary in support of character education. As part of this demonstration of virtues, staff worked to develop positive relationships with pupils, displaying kindness and empathy.

Returning to the *Teacher Education* project, Student Teachers were also asked about the extent to which they felt prepared for developing pupils' character. Chart 3.2 shows that 4.3% of respondents reported that they felt 'Very Prepared', and 20% felt 'Prepared', to develop the character of the pupils in their classrooms in the initial survey. In contrast, the post survey revealed that 15.8% felt 'Very Prepared', with the majority of respondents reporting that they felt 'Prepared' (51.3%) (Arthur et al., 2018a).

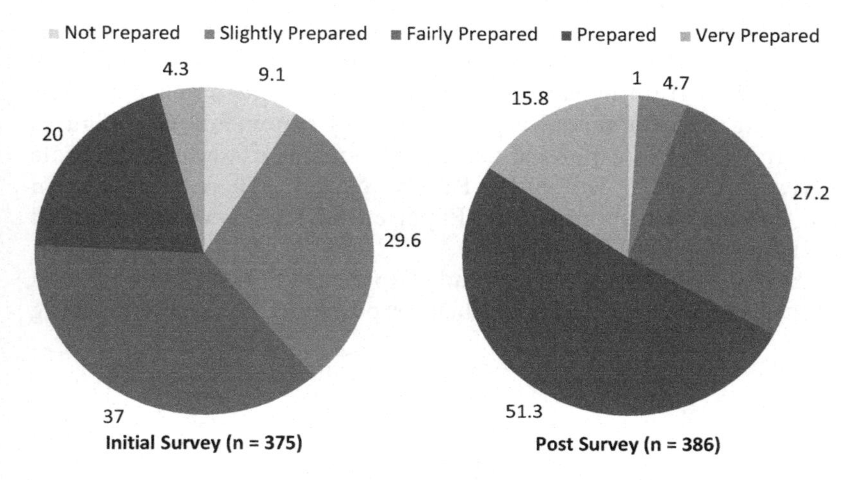

Chart 3.2 How Prepared Do You Feel to Develop the Character of the Pupils in Your Classroom?

Further analysis of this data found there to be a statistically significant[1] difference between the percentage of student teachers who reported being 'Very Prepared' or 'Prepared' between the initial survey and the post survey (24.3% initial survey; 67.1% post survey). Furthermore, statistically significant differences were also found within primary and secondary cohorts. Primary student teachers moved from 20.4% in the initial survey to 71.7% in the post survey, whereas secondary student teachers moved from 27.5% to 63.5% between the two surveys (Arthur et al., 2018a).

Virtuous practice and the workplace

Appreciating how the workplace impacts on teachers' professional practice is important for any meaningful exploration of virtue and character in teaching. *The Good Teacher* project examined responses to both questionnaire and interview data in order to describe the factors teachers reported as supporting and hampering them in being the kind of teacher they wished to be. Three themes emerged in the analysis: the extent to which teachers felt supported and motivated by their school and colleagues to work in ways they themselves valued, the emotional attachment they felt to their work and the pressures of time and stress they encountered. Section 4 of the *The Good Teacher* project's questionnaire asked NQTs to think about their training environment, and Experienced Teachers their working environment. Respondents read statements (see Figures 3.1 and 3.2) and responded using a 5-point Likert-style rating scale (Always, Mostly, Not Sure, Rarely, Never). 170 responses from NQTs and 110 responses from Experienced Teachers were analysed (Arthur et al., 2017).

Student Teachers, NQTs and Experienced Teachers spoke in largely positive terms about their respective training and working

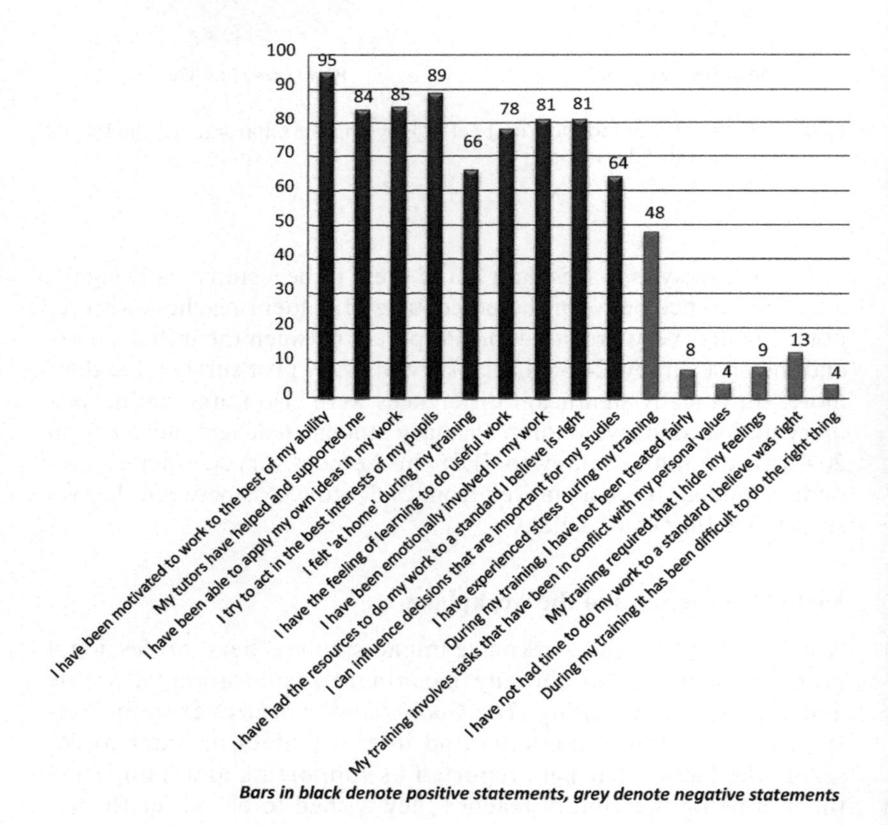

Figure 3.1 NQT 'Always' and 'Mostly' Responses to Workplace Conditions Questions (%). Bars in black denote positive statements, grey denote negative statements.

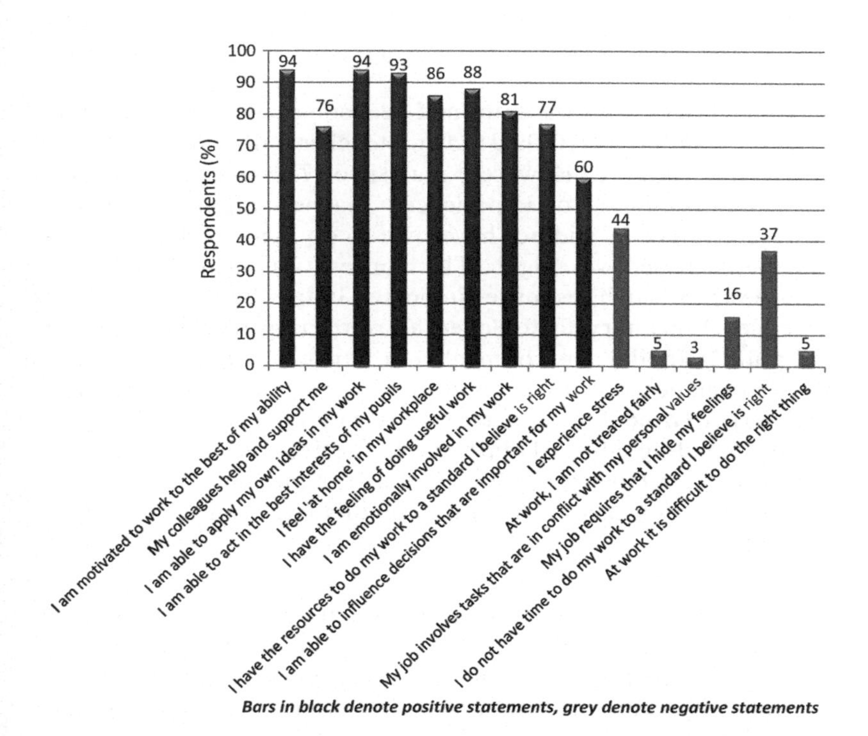

Figure 3.2 Experienced Teacher 'Always' and 'Mostly' Responses to Workplace Conditions Questions (%). Bars in black denote positive statements, grey denote negative statements.

environments. In some instances, this enthusiasm was also evidenced in interviews:

> You know that you're with a group of people that truly do love the profession, but also stay up to date with it and get the newest training where possible, so not just resting on their 10 years' experience; they're constantly updating their toolkit. So being at this school, I know that I'm going to be around really inspiring members of staff, both professionally and for the students, I'm going to witness some fantastic teaching practice. *Stdt Tchr*

> I think personally it's where I've worked and the people I've worked with, in that I think I've been lucky, I've always been encouraged to, I've never been sort of, oh, here's a scheme of work, you must follow it rigidly, this is what we're doing, this is how we're doing it, I've been

> allowed the freedom to be creative, to try things out on my own, I've been encouraged to do training and do different things. *Exp Tchr*

These findings are encouraging and bear some similarity to the findings of the OfSTED (2019a) study on teacher well-being considered earlier in Chapter 2. However, analysis of *The Good Teacher* data also found that 37% of Experienced Teachers reported that they 'always' or 'mostly' did not have time to do their work to a standard they believed was 'right'. This concern was also voiced in the interviews in which responses indicated limited space for virtuous practice. A primary factor cited as restricting teacher work was the political/policy environment – in particular, the focus placed on performance, attainment and assessment. Across the interviews with Experienced Teachers, a range of interconnected policy initiatives, including OFSTED inspection, the Teachers' Standards and performance related pay, were cited as threatening good practice. The sense of concern was captured by this Experienced Teacher in her interview:

> You have an over-emphasis on slavish assessment levels and artificial sub-division of levels and it's only through the confidence of good leadership at school level that you can stand against this regime. So again, we come back to the key principles of intelligence and confident leadership. Now, my intelligence and confident leadership gives me the space and the trust to get on. When that door is shut, I know that I am trusted to get on with the job and that they will stand between me and any unwarranted criticism, right, but if I didn't have that confident leadership, then I would feel completely exposed and I would be delivering a structured, formulaic, rigid programme of learning. *Exp Tchr*

Although this section focuses mainly on the perspectives of Experienced Teachers, it is worth noting that it was not just Experienced Teachers who expressed concerns regarding policy initiatives and inspection regimes, as the following two extracts from an NQT and a Student Teacher demonstrate:

> I think, as a trainee, it didn't affect me as much because I could kind of experiment with what I wanted to do, but in terms of teaching, it was you must constantly check, you must show what OFSTED want, instead of getting students to engage with the subject, and doing projects and activities, you will need to show

> progress every time because that's what OFSTED want you to do to account for stuff. *NQT*

> The Government at the moment, they're telling us to do all these things, but those are people that are telling us to do them that aren't teachers, that they don't know what it's like on a day-to-day basis. *Stdt Tchr*

Experienced Teachers in *The Good Teacher* project reported that collegiality and strong, supportive leadership within their schools enabled, or at least helped, them to cope with the pressures and stresses induced by the political and policy context. Indeed, having the support of colleagues was a strong theme in the interviews, whether framed as part of a mentoring relationship, sharing best practice and knowledge, or otherwise. Similarly, analysis of the questionnaire data found that 84% of NQTs and 76% of Experienced Teachers reported that they always or mostly felt supported by their colleagues, a sentiment echoed in a number of interviews:

> Your colleagues, I think, working with likeminded intellectual, dynamic, inspired individuals helps you to be that kind of teacher. *Exp Tchr*

Teachers at each career stage expressed concerns over their workload and at the impact workload pressures had on the development of their teaching practice. Questionnaire data revealed that 37% of Experienced Teachers reported not having adequate time to complete their work. As one Experienced Teacher explained in their interview, workload pressures focused on targets and assessment detracted from planning and teaching:

> I think also the workloads being excessive, data, which I hate, I can see the value of it but only in reason, and my school, that I've now left, was fixated on data as the answer to everything. So I think anything like that, where I didn't feel like I was able to plan lessons and teach, 'cause I was spending my whole time inputting data about national curriculum levels, when I wanted to really be planning lessons. *Exp Tchr*

This situation was not lost on Student Teachers who predicted that workload would be an issue and observed colleagues in school placements suffering the effects of excessive workload.

The formation of the 'good' teacher

In *The Good Teacher* project, the interviews asked respondents how they believed their education had prepared them for being the kind of teacher they wished to be as well as what advice they would offer to improve the education of beginning and experienced teachers. When respondents reflected on their aspirations as teachers, these were framed broadly in virtue-based terms, for example, wanting to be kind, honest or fair. The project also sought to explore how experiences in Initial Teacher Education (ITE) and Continuing Professional Development (CPD) might have contributed to laying the foundations for developing professional virtue and, perhaps most significantly, practical wisdom.

It is, perhaps, unsurprising that the dominant theme throughout Student Teachers' and NQTs' interviews was the practical and technical skills and techniques needed to manage the classroom. Student Teachers and NQTs were most concerned with meeting the Teachers' Standards and preparing for/handling the reality of the classroom and wider school environments. For this reason, in the interviews, there was a tendency for respondents to refer to performance virtues, such as resilience and perseverance, when describing the character strengths required for teaching as well as those to be cultivated in pupils. This might also be suggestive that attention to morality and character – both of teachers themselves and of pupils – might be lacking in initial teacher education and the continuing professional development of teachers more widely.

In the more recent *Teacher Education* project, the initial survey of student teachers (n = 369) examined their familiarity with the term 'character education'. Analysis of the responses found that at that stage of their ITE course, nearly two-thirds (64.9%) of the student teachers were not familiar with the term, with just over a quarter (27.4%) reporting having heard of the term but not knowing what it meant. Only a small percentage of responses (7.7%) reported that they were familiar with the term and knew its meaning. These figures are not dissimilar from those found in a Populus poll commissioned by the Jubilee Centre (2017) that surveyed qualified teachers (n = 457). That poll found that 55.8% were not familiar with the term character education, that 33.7% were familiar, but did not know what it means and that 10.5% were familiar and knew what it meant. These results can be considered alongside figures reported by the DfE (2017) which found that 37% of schools (n = 880) were 'familiar' with *character education*, 17% were 'familiar but did not know what it meant' and 46% were 'not familiar' (see Chart 3.3).

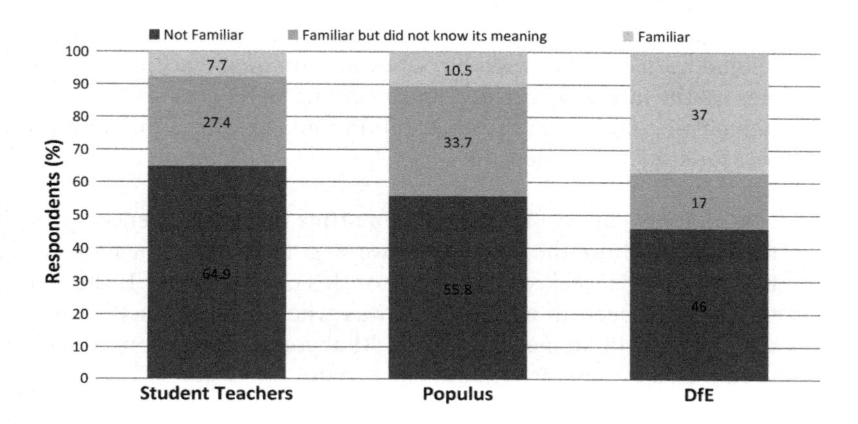

Chart 3.3 Familiarity with the Term *Character Education.*

While character education is not, of course, the only approach to moral education, given its recent revival in academic literature and the attention paid to it within educational policy circles in recent years, taken collectively these findings paint a somewhat negative snapshot of awareness of, and familiarity with, moral education within the teaching profession.

A significant strength of ITE courses lies in the partnerships between universities and schools, and a core role in this partnership is that of the school-based mentor. Over at least the last two decades, research literature on initial teacher education has pointed to the significance of good, positive mentoring on early career teachers (Arthur, Davison and Lewis, 2005; LoCasale-Crouch et al., 2012; Richter et al., 2013). Just as the Experienced Teachers (as mentioned above) had referred to the importance of mentoring and collegiality, so too the importance of good mentoring was highlighted in the interviews with Student Teachers and NQTs. Student Teachers reported that they valued mentors who understood their concerns, who promoted their professional development and who were able to relate learning to the individual student. It was clear from the interviews, however, that the quality of experience on placement varied and was often largely dependent on the quality and capacities of individual mentors. As one NQT reflected:

> I think the issue's really been, from what I've heard other people say, has been with mentors who have not really been, not really remembered what it's like to be starting out and making mistakes. *NQT*

In interviews, Experienced Teachers raised concerns about the pressure on Student Teachers, given the extent and ways in which aspects of ITE had been compromised by policy initiatives and accountability regimes. In the following extract, an Experienced Teacher spoke about the impact of time pressures on mentors and the effect this had on support for student teachers:

> I think more support from, and more time from, experienced professionals. I think the trainee that we've got with us at the moment has one hour a week with his mentor. It's crazy, isn't it? If the last time you've been in a classroom was when you, yourself, was a student aged 18, to me, that's crazy, that you have one hour a week to talk to a professional about what to do. *Exp Tchr*

These findings connect to other existing studies on stress, time pressures and workload pressures faced by teachers (Ball, 2008; Loonstra, Brouwers and Tomic, 2009; Skaalvik and Skaalvik, 2010, 2011; Green, 2011; Pietarinen et al., 2013) and seem to emphasise that such pressures also take a toll on the possibilities for, and depth of, mentoring.

The Good Teacher and the *Schools of Virtue* projects both highlighted the importance of a whole school ethos in developing character. The value of a positive and productive whole school ethos came through in the interviews of *The Good Teacher* project, for example, when NQTs discussed the factors that had supported them in becoming a good teacher. In these positive cases, schools were framed in terms of being a learning community. Such schools were also described as having a positive emphasis on reflection and on CPD in ways that helped the professional learning and development of early career teachers. As one NQT reported, working in a supportive learning environment was an important aspiration:

> I'd like to be in a school that has good support as well. Lots of, mainly, sharing practices with people in the department, and other departments, so that I can become a better teacher by learning from other people, rather than being by myself. *NQT*

To add a further perspective, *The Good Teacher* study also sought the views of Teacher Educators, who were asked about their views on the place and role of character in ITE. For these respondents, character was reported as being important both for good teaching and for being a good teacher. Perhaps not unsurprisingly, Teacher Educators highlighted the importance of character in selecting applicants for their ITE courses. Notably, however, the sorts of strengths commonly cited within the interviews focused on either personality traits (such as self-confidence) or on developing performance virtues (such as resilience). Furthermore, while committed to the importance of character within teaching, a small number of respondents raised questions about both the desirability and the practical possibility that teacher educators should have a role in developing the character of student teachers, a finding that strikes a chord with Sanger and Osguthorpe's (2011, 2013) contention that teacher preparation programmes often lack the language of the moral work of teaching.

Similarly to the teachers involved in the sample, Teacher Educators also spoke about the pressures on time and how these pressures restricted and prohibited sufficient attention on developing moral character. Instead, and as the following extract highlights, the priority was on achieving the relevant outcomes from the Teachers' Standards:

> We try and cram so much into less than a year that you can see why it wouldn't be addressed because we've got to help the trainees to meet the Teachers' Standards and a lot of that is about subject knowledge; but I think when you unpick what makes a good teacher, for me, it is some of those not so obvious characteristics that we need to help them to better understand. *Tchr Edcr*

Where Teacher Educators did talk about the development of student teachers' character strengths, the emphasis again remained largely on particular forms of professional behaviour, such as their attitude and commitment to working hard, the way they dressed and the way they conveyed themselves. In terms of learning processes, two were emphasised in particular: the modelling of behaviour (including by themselves as Teacher Educators) and the development of reflective practitioners. With regard to the former, the intention conveyed by some Teacher Educators was not for role models to be copied but for student teachers to incorporate positive aspects within their own practice. For example:

> You can't change who you are as a person, so the ones who are most outgoing and you know, all singing, all dancing, that's fine, but somebody else might see another teacher like that and go, I can never be that person. No, you can't be that person, but are there some aspects that you can actually incorporate into your own practice and use in your own practice. *Tchr Edcr*

With regard to the latter, reflection and evaluation typically focused on student teachers' practice – on what worked, what didn't work and why – rather than on their character *per se*:

> I'm a stickler as a tutor for things like professional appearance and punctuality, attendance, all that sort of thing, you hope send out subliminal messages, you know, if somebody's phone goes off, you can say to them, have you ever heard my phone ring in a session, so that, you know, we must practice what we preach. *Tchr Edcr*

> We try and push forward the character skills linked to resilience, adaptability, flexibility, interpersonal skills and communication, so that is probably constantly fed through. *Tchr Edcr*

Conclusion

The data presented in this chapter provides further evidence to the existing literature surveyed in the previous chapter that teachers do perceive themselves as having a moral role both in the sense that teaching is an ethical vocation and in the terms of forming pupils' character. In addition, as other studies (for example, Perryman and Calvert, 2019) have found, the Jubilee Centre's research confirms that ideas of making a difference to pupils' lives, working with young people, being a positive role model and shaping young people's character play an important role in motivating entrants to the teaching profession. While these findings are positive and should be welcomed, the data also gives pause for thought. The data also suggests that the conditions under which teachers work put pressure on them to maintain this motivation and enthusiasm (see also Kidger et al., 2016). So too, certain pervasive working conditions and practices within the teaching profession detract from the ethical work of teachers, leading to an emphasis on performance virtues such as determination and perseverance. Within such a context, the finding from *The Good Teacher* report that, for some respondents, colleagues provide support and in some ways ameliorate the stress of demands stands out, and highlights the importance of positive, collaborative relationships for good teaching (see also OfSTED, 2019a).

Note

1 ($p = 0.00 < \alpha\ 0.05$).

4 Teachers of character

Personal and ideal character strengths and responses to ethical dilemmas

Introduction

In this chapter we examine and discuss empirical data drawn from Jubilee Centre projects – *The Good Teacher* and *Teacher Education* – which have examined how teachers at various stages of their career – Student Teacher, Newly Qualified Teacher and Experienced Teacher – conceive their own personal character strengths and those character strengths they identify with the 'ideal' or 'good' teacher. In addition, drawing on data collected by *The Good Teacher* project, we present analysis of responses to a series of ethical dilemmas given by teachers at various stages of their career. Analysis of the dilemma data found that while the majority of teachers can confidently apply moral virtues when making professional decisions, there are some situations where this is challenging (particularly in situations where virtues conflict). Data analysis also suggested some significant differences in response based on career stage and gender.

The character strengths of teachers

As set out in the introduction to this book, both *The Good Teacher* project and the *Teacher Education* project sought respondents' views on their own personal character strengths as well as those they equated with the 'ideal' (*The Good Teacher* project) or 'good' (*Teacher Education* project) teacher. For both projects, respondents were given a list of 24 character strengths from which to choose to describe their personal character and that of the ideal/good teacher. In *The Good Teacher* project, the 24 character strengths were taken from the VIA's list of 24 character strengths.[1] In the *Teacher Education* project, a different set of 24 character strengths were used (though some strengths do appear in both lists). These character strengths were composed in connection to the Jubilee Centre's four building blocks of character and contained six character strengths for each of the blocks – moral, intellectual, civic and performance. As the two projects employed two different sets of 24 character strengths, it is difficult to make direct comparisons between the data. For this reason, in this section we present the data from the two projects separately while also drawing out some findings common to both.

A core aim of *The Good Teacher* study, then, was to investigate (1) how Student Teachers, Newly Qualified Teachers, and Experienced Teachers conceived their own character strengths and (2) how these conceptions of their own character strengths compared with their descriptions of the character strengths needed by the 'ideal' teacher. As can be seen in Figure 4.1, for the teachers in *The Good Teacher* project the six most-cited personal character strengths were fairness (55%), honesty (50%), humour (50%), kindness (49%), love of learning (44%) and creativity (41%). These most-cited reported personal character traits have some overlap with those most commonly cited by the teachers as being constitutive of the 'ideal' teacher: fairness (78%), creativity (68%), love of learning (61%), humour (53%), perseverance (45%) and leadership (40%). Four character strengths – fairness, humour, love of learning and creativity – appeared in the top six most cited on both the personal character strengths reported by teachers and those they identified with the 'ideal' teacher. Two character strengths in the top six personal strengths – honesty and kindness – did not feature in the top six for the 'ideal' teacher, while two in the top six of the 'ideal' teacher – perseverance and leadership – did not feature on the list of personal strengths reported. Though individual respondents may have had different reasons for the difference between their personal and ideal strengths, it is noteworthy that the two strengths that appeared in the top six of the personal but not the ideal – honesty and kindness – were moral virtues, while the two that appeared in the top six of the ideal but not the personal – perseverance and leadership – were performance virtues.

Analysis of the data also found, as demonstrated in Figure 4.2, that there was a strong degree of commonality between Student Teachers, NQTs and Experienced Teachers in the six highest reported personal character strengths. Student Teachers and NQTs identified the same six personal character strengths – fairness, honesty, kindness, humour, love of learning, and creativity – while five of these (all expect love of learning) were also selected by Experienced Teachers whom also included perseverance.

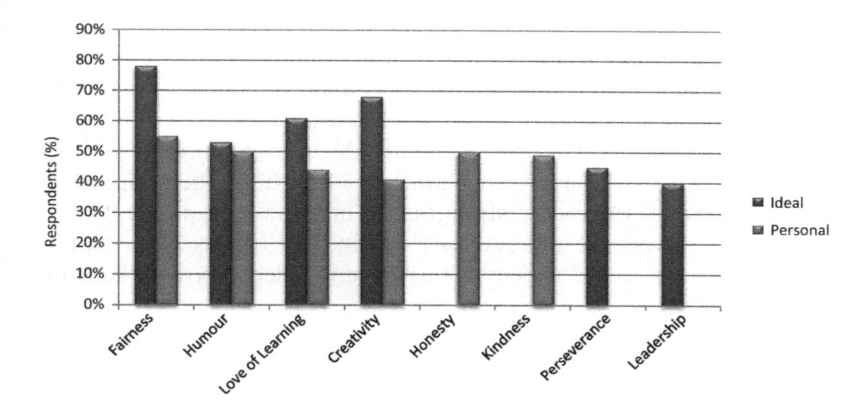

Figure 4.1 Comparison of Reported Character Strength: Personal and for the 'Ideal' Teacher (%).

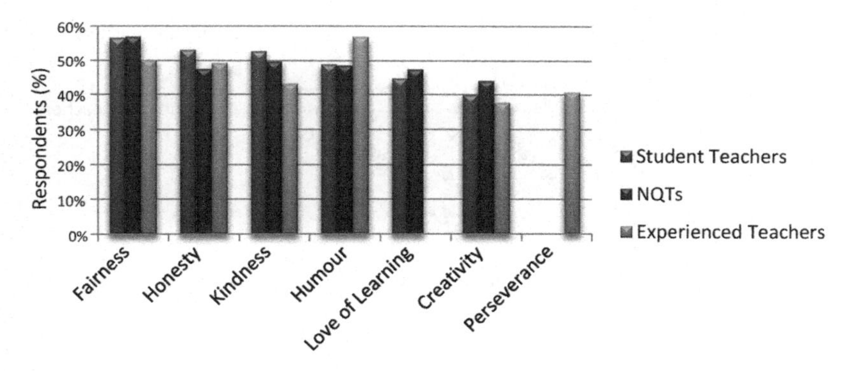

Figure 4.2 Top Six Reported Personal Character Strengths (%).

When we turn to the top six reported character strengths of the 'ideal' teacher, and as shown in Figure 4.3, analysis of the data found that despite their being considerable overlap of opinion regarding the top six character strengths for the 'ideal' teacher, some differences across career stages also existed. The five character strengths of fairness, creativity, love of learning, humour and perseverance appeared in the top six character strengths of the 'ideal' teachers reported by Student Teachers, NQTs and Experienced Teachers. However, Student Teachers identified leadership (53%), NQTs teamwork (45%) and Experienced Teachers social intelligence (36%) and honesty (36%) within their top six, respectively. Using 2-way analysis of variance (ANOVA) tests, followed by Kruskal Wallis or Mann Whitney tests, some differences in responses regarding *all* 24 character strengths reached a level of statistical significance.

Similarities between the top six personal character strengths reported by male and female respondents were also found. As Figure 4.4 shows, male and female respondents both reported four strengths – fairness, kindness, honesty and humour – as within their top six reported personal character strengths. While male respondents also included perseverance and curiosity within their top six reported personal character strengths, female respondents selected love of learning and creativity.

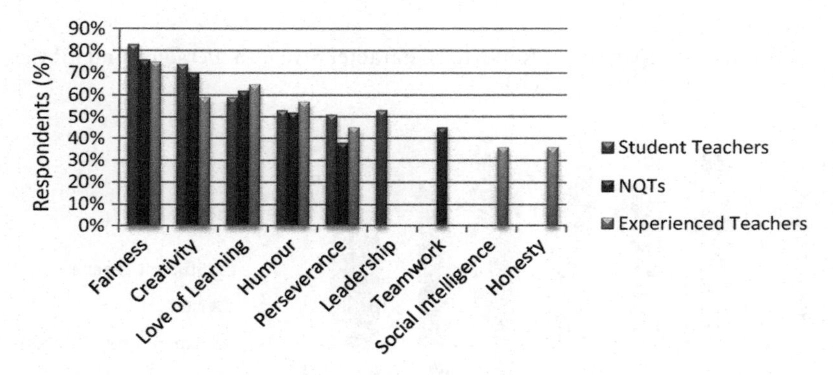

Figure 4.3 Top Six Reported Character Strengths for the 'Ideal' Teacher (%).

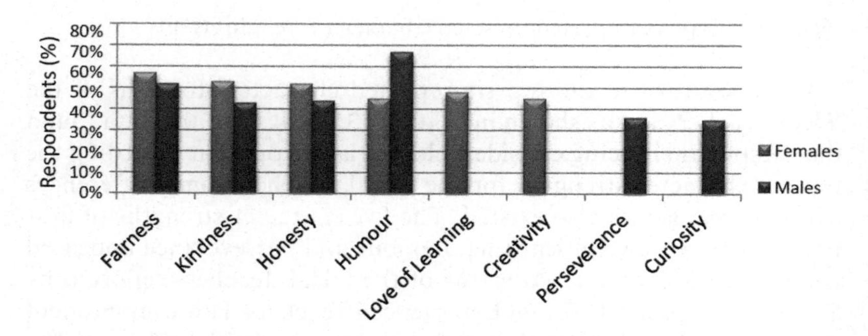

Figure 4.4 Top Six Reported Personal Character Strengths, by Gender (%).

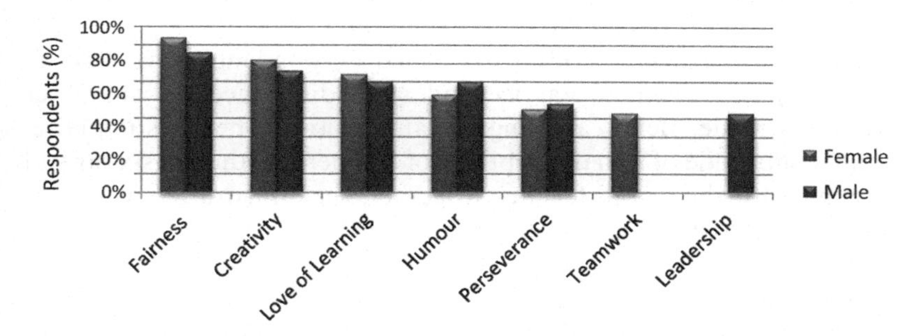

Figure 4.5 Reported Character Strengths for the 'Ideal' Teacher, by Gender (%).

With regard to the reported character strengths for the 'ideal' teacher, and as highlighted in Figure 4.5, male and female respondents both included the following five character strengths within the top six reported character strengths of the 'ideal' teacher: fairness, creativity, love of learning, humour and perseverance. The only difference between the top six reported strengths of the 'ideal' teacher was that male respondents reported leadership to be sixth most important while female respondents selected teamwork.

The Good Teacher study also examined the personal character strengths of teachers through the use of interviews. Analysis of the interview data found that respondents typically discussed their personal character strengths in terms of three broad themes:

- performance virtues, such as resilience and organisational abilities;
- virtues that contribute to positive relationships, such as empathy, fairness and being approachable and;
- virtues that reflected emotional dispositions, such as passion, enthusiasm and love (of subject or children).

It is interesting to note that although they did not feature highly in the questionnaire exercise, performance virtues such as perseverance (ranked seventh) and self-regulation (eighteenth) frequently featured in respondents' discourse in interviews. That performance virtues came through more strongly in the interview data reflects the way that in the interviews teachers described the virtues *they sought to develop in their students*. This recognition is not to say that performance virtues dominated; indeed, across the interviews, frequent reference was made to the virtues of patience, trust and care.

The Good Teacher study also asked respondents how character strengths influence practice and what difference the character strengths made. Below are single examples from the questionnaire, from a multitude of rich descriptions of teachers, of the top six ranked strengths for the 'good' teacher. Together, they illustrate how entangled the different character strengths are in practice:

Fairness: Ranging from the way she maximised learning for everyone, listened to everyone's concerns and acted on them to justify her decision-making processes and reprimands.

Creativity: She loved learning and instilled a sense of the value and joy of it by planning creative and interesting lessons even for the most apparently dull subjects.

Love of learning: She was passionate about her subject, which showed in the ways she constantly drew our attention to curiosities of French language and culture, her resourcefulness, her enthusiasm for teaching us.

Humour: He also has a fantastic sense of humour, allowing the class to have fun and enjoy their time in the classroom, but knowing when it was time for serious work.

Perseverance: Her perseverance becomes evident particularly with the lower ability students where she constantly aims to think of new ways to teach topics that these students find difficult to grasp.

Leadership: The teacher I am thinking of created a classroom environment that felt like she was in control and held the space yet gave the students a sense of space and room for them to explore and learn.

The study also examined whether the Experienced Teachers believed that the character strengths needed to be a good teacher had changed during the period they had been teaching. Here, opinion was divided. Some Experienced Teachers reported that the strengths needed in teaching today were the same as when they had started their teaching careers, while other Experienced Teachers argued that occupational and social conditions had changed the priorities for teachers' characters.

Analysis of the data drawn from Experienced Teachers highlighted two further notable themes that connect to the nature of teaching today. The first was the ability to reflect, and the value of reflecting, on one's practice and recognising that teaching was a lifelong project of learning and adapting. The second, in contrast, was the degree of surveillance and control that exists over individual practice. For example, one Experienced Teacher commented:

> We were having to do lesson plans for every lesson: there were observations, no notice observations and so on, and that just creates a very different atmosphere; but also, the kind of teaching that they're looking for, this very reductive, programmatic, follow this model, those are different kinds of traits that we'll need, rather than the era when I started. *Exp Tchr*

These sentiments highlight the influence of occupational context and policy in creating systems where certain character strengths typically associated with 'the professional' – such as judgement or autonomy – may be viewed as being undermined or as of less importance than others, particularly those that may be perceived as needed to manage the various demands on teachers' work.

The *Teacher Education* project also examined the 'personal' character strengths of respondents and those they associated with a 'good' teacher. As well as employing a different set of 24 character strengths, this project sought two different types of response regarding the character strengths – ratings and rankings. In their questionnaire responses, student teachers were asked to *rate* 24 character strengths from 1 to 7, first in terms of their personal character strengths and then in terms of those strengths which characterised a 'good' teacher. As Chart 4.1 illustrates, when asked to rate 24 character strengths from 1 to 7 depending on how each described their own character, the mean rating score for 23 out of the 24 character strengths increased between the initial and post questionnaires, with the largest increases in mean rating score being for community awareness, resilience, reflection, citizenship, confidence and resourcefulness.

Further analysis showed statistically significant increases between the initial survey and post survey mean rating scores for 16 of the 24 personal character strengths (highlighted in Chart 4.1 with *). Of the eight character strengths in which no statistically significant change was observed, five were moral character strengths, two were civic and one was intellectual.

Student teachers' ratings of both their personal character strengths and the character strengths of a 'good' teacher were each separated into the Four Building Blocks of Character. Chart 4.2 depicts how in

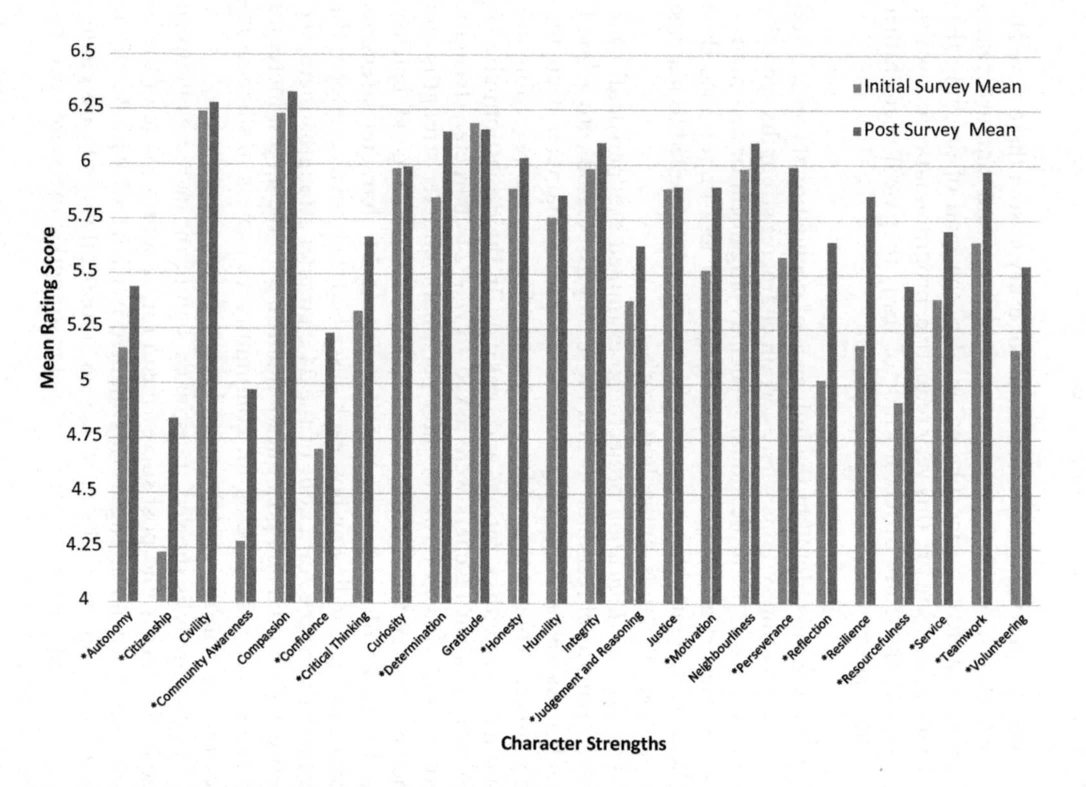

Chart 4.1 Student Teachers' Personal Character Strengths.

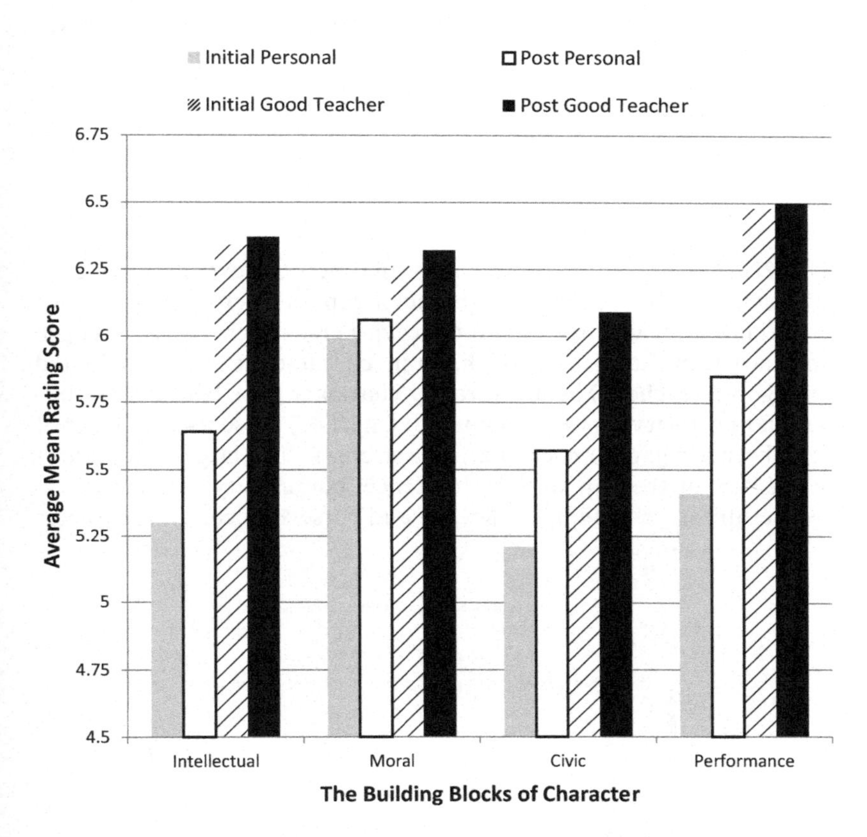

Chart 4.2 Character Strength Ratings Separated into the Building Blocks of Character.

both the initial and post surveys, personal character strengths were rated in the following order:

1 Moral
2 Performance
3 Intellectual
4 Civic

Further analysis revealed statistically significant increases between the initial and post survey average means for performance, civic and intellectual character strengths. In both the initial survey and post survey, student teachers' ratings of what they consider to be the character strengths of a 'good' teacher were rated in the following order (Arthur et al., 2018a):

1 Performance
2 Intellectual
3 Moral
4 Civic

The *Teacher Education* project also analysed the extent to which a 'character gap' was evident. A character gap represents the difference between the mean rating score for each personal character strength and the mean rating score of the same character strength attributed to a 'good' teacher. The mean rating character gaps between the initial and post surveys were compared. Chart 4.3 presents the extent of this character gap for each character strength. The largest reductions in the size of the gap were in resilience, community awareness, resourcefulness, reflection, confidence and perseverance. The character

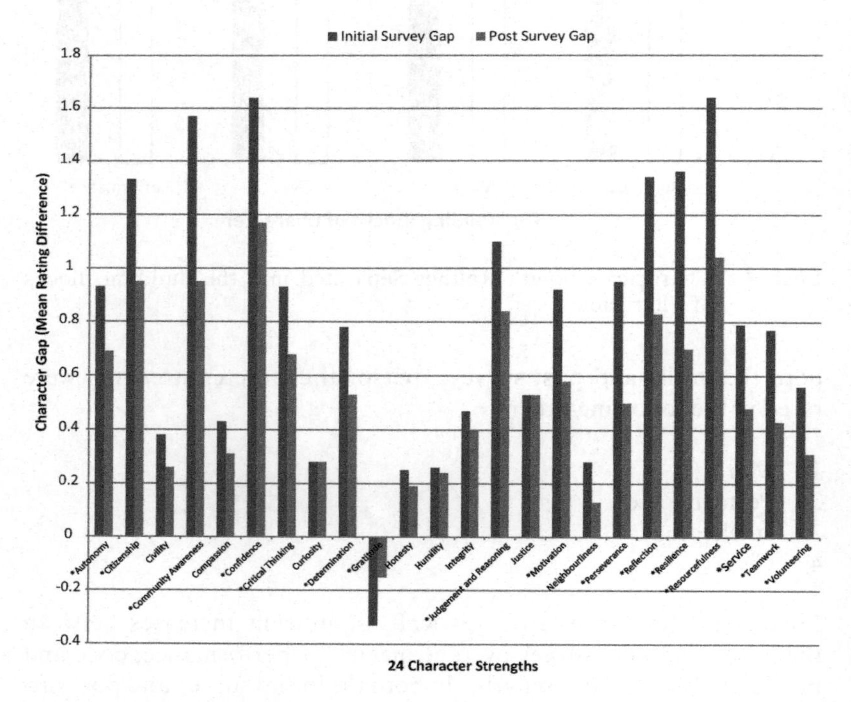

Chart 4.3 Character Gap Comparison.

strengths with the largest character gaps at the post survey were confidence, resourcefulness, community awareness, citizenship, judgement and reasoning and reflection (Arthur et al., 2018a).

Further analysis showed that in both the initial and post survey, the character gap for each of the 24 character strengths was statistically significant. For 16 of the 24 character strengths (highlighted in Chart 4.3 with *), the reduction of the gap between the two points in time was statistically significant. Of the eight character strengths in which no statistically significant change was observed, five were moral character strengths, two were civic and one was intellectual (Arthur et al., 2018a).

In addition to rating the character strengths, respondents in the *Teacher Education* were asked to pick and *rank* the six character strengths which best described their own personal character, placing the strongest first. Analysis of these responses showed a congruence between the initial survey and post survey for the character strengths of compassion, honesty and determination (see Chart 4.4). In contrast, between the initial and post surveys the character strengths of integrity, civility, curiosity and gratitude (note here that in the initial survey seven character strengths are reported as curiosity and gratitude both had a ranking of 5.7%) were replaced in the highest rated six by motivation, resilience and teamwork. In the initial survey, the top-rated character strengths consisted of four moral character strengths, one

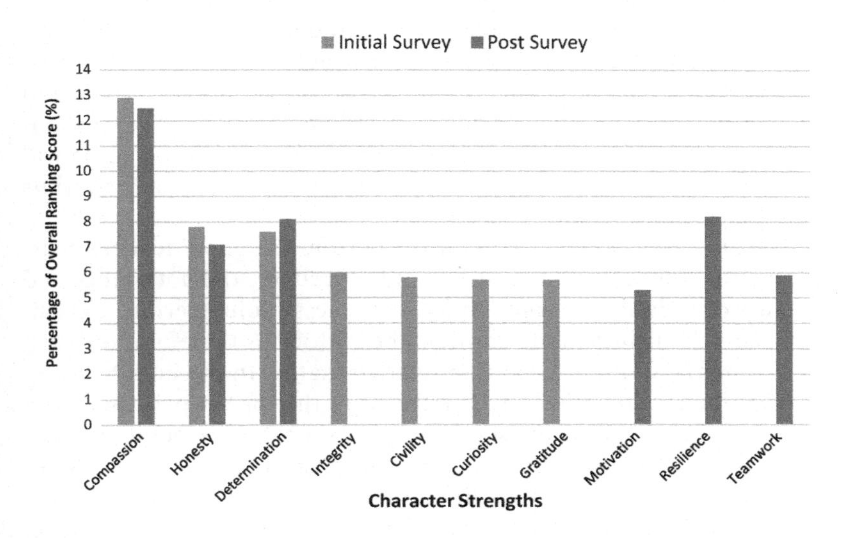

Chart 4.4 Overall Ranking Score of the Top Six Personal Character Strengths.

performance, one civic and one intellectual. In the post survey the top six consisted of one moral character strength, three performance, two intellectual and no civic. The increased prevalence of the performance character strengths in the post pre-service teacher education experience is notable.

The analysis also revealed that the bottom six personal character strengths in the initial survey and post survey did not change and comprised: community awareness, citizenship, service, judgement and reasoning, volunteering and resourcefulness. The lowest rated six personal character strengths for both the initial and post surveys therefore consisted of four civic and two intellectual character strengths. Analysis of this data also evidenced statistically significant increases between the initial survey and post survey with regard to six character strengths: citizenship, confidence, perseverance, reflection, resilience and teamwork. Statistically significant decreases existed for six character strengths: civility, gratitude, humility, justice, neighbourliness and volunteering (Arthur et al., 2018a).

In a similar vein to *The Good Teacher* project, in the initial survey and post survey, student teachers were asked to pick and rank the six character strengths which best described a 'good' teacher, placing the strongest first (again remembering that the *Teacher Education* project used 24 character strengths drawn from the Jubilee Centre's 4 building blocks). In the analysis of these responses, similarity was found for all of the top six ranked 'good' teacher character strengths in the initial survey and post survey[2] with teamwork being added to the top ranked character strengths in the post survey (see Chart 4.5). In the initial survey, the top six consisted of one moral character strength, three performance and two intellectuals. In the post survey, the top six consisted of one moral character strength, four performance and two intellectuals (Arthur et al., 2018a).

The analysis also revealed that the bottom six 'good' teacher character strengths in the initial survey and post survey did not change and comprised: gratitude, community awareness, volunteering, citizenship, neighbourliness and humility. The bottom six therefore consisted of two moral and four civic character strengths. In the initial survey, two character strengths were congruent in the top six personal character strengths and the top six character strengths of a 'good' teacher: compassion and determination. In the post survey four character strengths were congruent in the top six personal character strengths and the top six character strengths of a 'good' teacher: compassion,

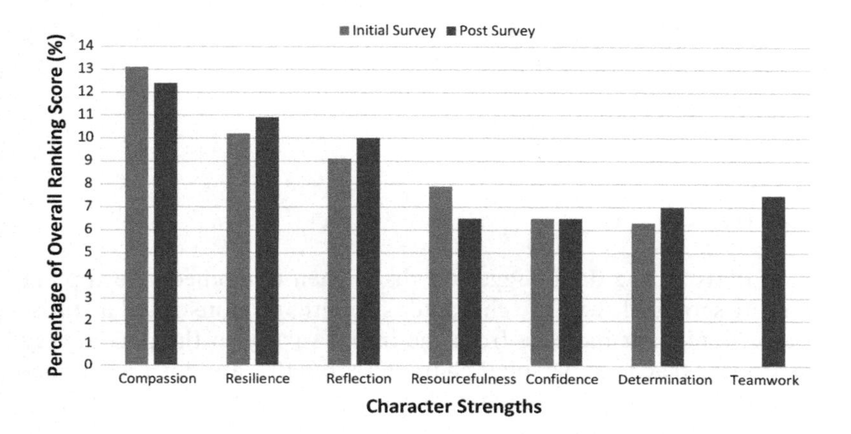

Chart 4.5 Overall Ranking Score for the Top Six 'Good' Teacher Character Strengths.

resilience, determination and teamwork. Volunteering, community awareness and citizenship featured in the bottom six ranked personal character strengths and the bottom six ranked character strengths of a 'good' teacher in both the initial survey and post survey (Arthur et al., 2018a).

Student teachers' ranking scores for both their top six personal character strengths and the top six character strengths of a 'good' teacher were each separated into the Building Blocks of Character. Chart 4.6 shows that in the initial survey, personal character strengths were ranked in this order:

1 Moral
2 Performance
3 Intellectual
4 Civic

In the post survey, personal character strengths were ranked in this order:

1 Performance
2 Moral
3 Intellectual
4 Civic

Chart 4.6 also shows that character strength rankings of a 'good' teacher did not change from the initial survey to the post survey. They were ranked in this order for both:

1 Performance
2 Intellectual
3 Moral
4 Civic

Analysis of the data suggested that, when combined, the top six ranking scores of the civic character strengths demonstrated a statistically significant increase from the initial survey to the post survey for student teachers' personal character strengths and for the character strengths of a 'good' teacher. When combined, the top six ranking scores of the moral character strengths demonstrated a statistically significant decrease from the initial survey to the post survey for student teachers' personal character strengths and for the character strengths of a 'good' teacher (Arthur et al., 2018a).

Data from the *Teacher Education* project found that the majority of student teachers believed that the development teachers' character was either 'Important' or 'Very Important' (see Chart 4.7). Interestingly, the perceived importance of developing teachers' character increased during the ITE year, with a higher percentage of respondents reporting that the development of teachers' character was 'Very Important' in the post survey (40.9%) compared to the initial survey

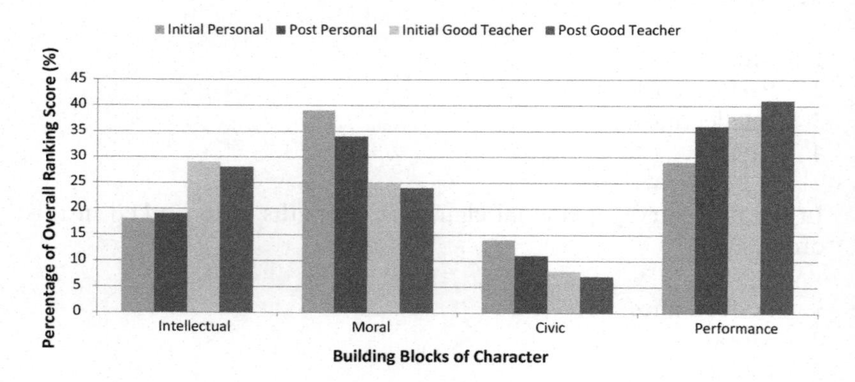

Chart 4.6 Ranking Scores of Character Strengths Separated into the Building Blocks of Character.

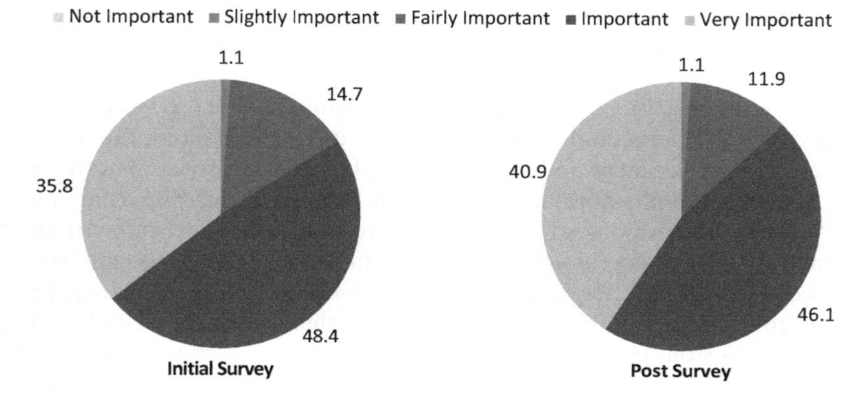

Chart 4.7 How Important Do You Think the Development of a Teacher's Character Is in Their Professional Development?

(35.8%) and a lower percentage of respondents reporting developing teachers' character to be 'Fairly Important' in the post survey (11.9%) compared to the initial survey (14.7%). It should also be noted that, in both the initial survey and post survey, no respondents considered the development of teachers' character to be 'Not Important'.

Further analysis of the *Teacher Education* project data indicated that, when comparing responses to both the initial survey and the post survey, there were statistically significant differences between student teachers undertaking courses in primary and secondary education. Student teachers on primary education ITE programmes had the highest proportion of 'Very Important' and 'Important' responses in the initial survey (88.2%) and post survey (93.5%) compared with student teachers on secondary education ITE programmes (initial survey 80.8%; post survey 81.9%). A statistically significant[3] difference was also found between the initial survey and post survey responses of primary student teachers who reported that the development of a teacher's character was 'Very Important' or 'Important'. Combined, these two responses increased from 88.2% to 93.5% between the initial survey and post survey.

Exploring virtue-based reasoning and judgement through the dilemmas

Across a number of Jubilee Centre projects, ethical dilemmas have been used as a data collection tool (see, for example, Arthur et al., 2015b,

2018b; Kristjánsson, 2017a, 2017b). In *The Good Teacher* study participants responded to a set of professional dilemmas (six dilemmas which explore the role of virtues and values in decision making, using scenarios and a scoring system created by, and piloted with, an expert panel[4] of over 40 practitioners and educators). Dilemmas were used as they (a) promise to offer a credible way to gain an insight into moral functioning and development and (b) can ideally be designed so as to activate more than simply moral reasoning skills (Kristjánsson, 2015, chap. 3). Nevertheless, responses to dilemmas serve as an indication, rather than guarantee, of action or understanding of moral sensitivity in a real, particular situation. They do not, in and by themselves, *measure* virtue, nor do any such definitive measures exist elsewhere, but when combined with data from interviews and self-reports, they may contribute to an overall understanding of virtue in professional practice.

The intention in employing the six dilemmas was not to seek a certain, pre-determined 'correct' response from respondents but was instead to ask respondents to explain their reasoning and the judgements arrived at with a particular focus on virtue-based reasoning. Each of the dilemmas focused on a particular challenge that raised competing professional demands on teachers. This said, two broad findings are initially noteworthy. The first is that for some dilemmas responses evidenced a high degree of similarity; there was, that is, a level of consensus about what course of action was deemed to be the best available in the given circumstances. In contrast, other dilemmas led to more variation in responses and reasons given. Those dilemmas about which respondents offered similar reasoning and judgements concerned curriculum flexibility, assessment and parents. Those where reasoning and judgements were more varied concerned school rules, teaching sensitive topics and working with colleagues. The second broad finding that is noteworthy from the outset is that little differences were found in overall responses between respondents at different career stages.

The six moral dilemmas used in *The Good Teacher* study are presented in full in Appendix Two. Here, we provide a brief precise of each and present the ways in which respondents reasoned about the issues raised in each dilemma and the judgements made:

The Curriculum Flexibility ('Snowy Afternoon') dilemma focused on whether teachers would be willing to be flexible in letting children experience snow in the schoolyard even where this meant interrupting a planned lesson. For some children, snow was a new phenomenon; hence, teachers had to choose between disrupting the lesson or ignoring the children's requests. The expert panel identified the dilemma as involving reasoning between options potentially associated with, on the one hand, the virtues of appreciation of beauty, love of learning, kindness and creativity and, on the other, perseverance, fairness and leadership.

Respondents exhibited a high degree of consensus about the most appropriate form of action, with 87% reporting that they would take the children outside to experience the snow. However, less consensus was discernible regarding the reasons given for taking that course of action. Reasons provided varied, with 38% of those who would take the children outside citing *the opportunity for some child-centred learning, to share experiences and learn from one another* as first choice most often, a reason associated with creativity by the expert panel. Less emphasis was placed on rules and consequences, with only a small percentage of respondents citing these as their first choice in reasoning through their decision – regardless of course of action chosen (5–11% rules and 7–13% consequences). In practice, of course, professional decisions frequently incorporate balancing rules, consequences and virtues, as the following reflection from an Experienced Teacher underlines:

> I would not have a problem at all with the children going out in the snow; but at schools that I've worked at, my last school, for example, we had to kind of keep them in during the snow, in case they had someone throw a snowball. So you've got to be aware of what your boss would want you to do too and so you're often kind of guided by that, rather than your own values anyway; you're guided by towing the party line really. *Exp Tchr*

A second dilemma focused on *School rules ('Uniform').* In this dilemma, respondents were faced with a child who persistently came to school in the wrong shoes but had difficult home circumstances that might have made it difficult for his family to afford the regulation shoes. The teacher had to choose between sending the child home or ignoring his wearing of the trainers. The expert panel identified the dilemma as involving reasoning between options potentially associated with, on the one hand, the virtues of fairness, perseverance, hope and kindness and, on the other, fairness, judgement, perspective and kindness. For this dilemma, responses showed less consensus on the chosen course of action, with 51% choosing to send the child home and 49% choosing to ignore the trainers. For those who choose to send the child home, one reason dominated the explanations of this choice – namely, *fairness to other students* (40%). Of those who choose to send the child home, 20% cited the need to uphold school rules as being part of their job, and none cited the consequence-based reason. For those respondents whose choice was to ignore that the child was wearing trainers, the most cited reason was *fairness in not wishing the child to miss lessons if they did not have other shoes to change in to* (64%). In the following, a Student Teacher describes why their decision was guided by fairness over an adherence to rules:

> I didn't refer to the standards, certainly not, when I was considering what I was going to do; because to be honest, if I think it's the right thing to do, so like for the shoes one in particular, asking why are you wearing trainers, 'is there a particular problem, 'blah de blah'?' I actually don't care if I meet the standards, to be honest. I think the best thing is to actually talk about it. *Stdt Tchr*

A third dilemma concentrated on assessment ('The Exam'), and more specifically, whether a junior teacher should join in with their Deputy Head who was helping students with an examination or should refuse to join in and challenge the senior colleague. The students being helped had been disadvantaged by staff absence earlier in the year. The expert panel identified the dilemma as involving reasoning between options potentially associated with, on the one hand, the virtues of fairness, social intelligence, perspective and hope and, on the other, fairness, leadership, self-regulation and honesty.

For this dilemma, respondents evidenced a high degree of consensus about the right course of action, with 97% choosing the option to *not help the students and challenge the Deputy Head about her actions after the exam*. Similarly to the Curriculum Flexibility dilemma, the high degree of consensus regarded the course of action did not translate into consensus regarding the main justification for such action. For this dilemma, rules were the main reason cited, with 26% of respondents returning this response. This approach was indicated in the following statement from an NQT:

> I immediately as a professional would have thought, no, actually, that's not fair and it's going against the assessment guidelines and exam boards. However, last week, I found myself in that exact same situation. *NQT*

The Working with Parents ('Parents' Evening') dilemma focused on an NQT who faced a challenge between maintaining confidentiality at a Parents' Evening or sharing other parents' concerns over distractions posed by a child with Special Educational Needs. The expert panel identified the dilemma as involving reasoning between options potentially associated with, on the one hand, the virtues of fairness, honesty, bravery and hope, and, on the other, prudence, perspective, judgement and kindness. Responses for this dilemma showed a strong sense of consensus about the appropriate course of action. Eighty-seven percent of respondents choose the option of *not discussing one pupil with another's parents at a parents' evening* and only 13% reported that they would choose to discuss the pupil with other parents. For this dilemma, rules seemed to play a larger role in underpinning the course of action. Thirty percent of teachers chose *the Teachers' Standards guide to communicate effectively with parents* as a primary reason for discussing the pupil, while 51% of teachers opted to *uphold school policy on confidentiality* as the primary reason for not discussing the pupil. Of course, this dilemma is one in which different rules (communicating effectively/maintaining confidentiality) from different sources (Teacher Standards/school policy) provide conflicting guidance, and it is notable that in arriving at their reported decisions, respondents tended to prioritise one set of rules over the other. This reliance on rules does not, however, necessarily mean that there is not considerable thought behind a decision:

> Sometimes, the powers that be need to know what the extenuating circumstances are, why people have acted the way they have. Because always, there's lots of layers every time, isn't there? *NQT*

The Teaching Sensitive or Controversial Topics dilemma concerned a situation in which a student was overheard making apparently racist comments following a citizenship lesson on the 'war on terror'. In this dilemma, respondents were asked whether, as the teacher, they would report the student or would not report the student and would instead tackle the issue in a subsequent lesson with the whole class. The expert panel identified the dilemma as involving reasoning between options potentially associated with, on the one hand, the virtues of bravery, prudence, kindness and courage, and, on the other, judgement, perspective, humility and hope.

For this dilemma, 57% of respondents suggested that they would report the student, with 43% choosing not to report student and to tackle the issue in a subsequent lesson. When respondents turned to their reasons, the most popular justification selected by those who would report the student concerned moral leadership, namely, *the need to act as a role model and be seen to be taking discrimination seriously* (31%). Thirty-nine percent of respondents who would choose to tackle the issue in a subsequent lesson cited that *this pupil's views may be shared by others in the class. Reporting just one pupil will not address the problem effectively* as the primary reason for acting. Interestingly, here, reasons given for the former course of action were more dispersed between virtue-based considerations and rule-based considerations than those reasons cited for the latter course of action in which rules and consequences hardly featured.

The *Relationships with Colleagues ('Staffroom Chat')* dilemma asked respondents what their course of action would be if, as a teacher, they regularly overheard a colleague making derogatory remarks about a class and commenting that (s)he did not bother preparing properly for their lessons because they were not worth it. The choice in this dilemma was between ignoring the comments, reporting the colleague or challenging them directly. This was the only dilemma in which three, rather than two, options were available. The expert panel identified the dilemma as involving reasoning between options potentially associated with (1) self-regulation, fairness, judgement and social intelligence; (2) self-regulation, teamwork, kindness and honesty; and (3) leadership, bravery, hope and prudence. Responses to this dilemma evidenced a spread across the three options. Fifteen percent of respondents stated that that they would opt to ignore the comments, 39% that they would report the colleague and 46% that they would challenge the colleague directly.

When the reasons given were analysed, the study found that the majority of respondents (64%) – and 81% of Experienced Teachers – who chose to ignore the comments prioritised the virtue-based justification, namely, that 'you do not know, for certain, what really happens in the classroom and the teacher may just be expressing their frustrations'. This pattern was repeated for those choosing to speak to a more senior member of staff about the teacher's comments. In addition, Student Teachers (44%) were more likely to report the colleague than either NQTs (39%) or Experienced Teachers (29%). Turning to the 46% of respondents who chose to challenge the teacher directly about their comments, there was a clear consistency across respondents from different career stages in terms of their reasons given. Notably, recourse to rules (reference to the Teachers' Standards) and consequences *(that additional scrutiny of teaching might follow)* played little part in the reported reasoning (3% and 0%, respectively). This suggests that, for the respondents in *The Good Teacher* study, virtue-based considerations played a much greater role in their reasoning over this dilemma than rules or consequences. That this is so highlights the challenges involved in arriving at decision about preferable course of action, requiring the employment of professional thinking, reflection and judgement. As one respondent in the study who was an Experienced Teacher contemplated:

> If you have a colleague who isn't doing the right thing and isn't pulling their weight and the students are complaining to you, it's really difficult to know what to do with it; because you don't want to be a snitch, you know and go to your Head of department or whatever, but if you speak to the colleague and the colleague then is dismissive and doesn't change or whatever, then I think there's a massive moral dilemma as to what you do with that and where you go. We've had that, which is really problematic and I still don't know really... *Exp Tchr*

Looking across the dilemmas

Through using dilemmas to elicit respondent's choices about, and justifications of, given courses of action in each of the situations, *The Good Teacher* study provides important insights about the types of reasons provided by respondents as well as similarities and differences between teachers at different stages of their careers (Student Teachers, NQTs and Experienced Teachers).

Analysis of the dilemma data found there to be large degrees of consistency between respondents across the career stages in their first-level reasoning to explain their chosen courses of action. In 8 of the 13 possible options, the same reason was cited most by respondents from each of the career stages. For one option (challenging the teacher directly) of one dilemma (relationships with colleagues), there was complete agreement in reasoning across respondents from all three career stages.

Further analysis was undertaken in order to assess whether patterns could be found in the reasoning of respondents. In particular, differences between career stages and genders were explored through two-way ANOVA tests and subsequent Mann Whitney U tests (see online at: www.jubileecentre.ac.uk/professions for details). Analysis showed that, for the respondents in *The Good Teacher* study, career stage *sometimes* has an influence on the likelihood of selecting either a consequence-based, rule-based or virtue-based reason. A number of these differences were significant at the 0.05 level. For example, for the *Relationships with Colleagues* dilemma, when opting to 'Speak to a more senior member of staff about the teacher's comments', NQTs were significantly more likely to select the consequence-based reason as compared to Student Teachers and Experienced Teachers. It appears that when faced with a dilemma that involves a colleague, NQTs more readily factor in the consequences of their behaviour, whereas Experienced Teachers place little weight on this aspect of reasoning.

Further analysis of the data found that, overall, the likelihood of selecting a rule-based, consequence-based or virtue-based justification was not significantly influenced by gender. However, there were some specific instances where gender did seem to influence responses. For example, in order to support their choice 'not to help the students and to challenge the Deputy Head about her actions after the exam', male respondents were more likely to select the consequence-based reason ($p = < 0.05$) 'if you do not stand up to her someone may find out there was cheating and you may get into trouble'. Similarly, there was one instance in which female respondents were more likely than males to select the rule-based reason; 'The "Teachers' Standards" state that a teacher should "communicate effectively with parents with regard to students" achievements and well-being'. This is an opportunity to do so'.

Overall, and across the dilemmas, NQTs and Experienced Teachers relied less on rule-based reasoning than Student Teachers. That this was the case may suggest that teachers at the early stages of their professional learning and development rely on rules to a greater extent than those with more professional experience in order to navigate ethical dilemmas and that this reliance may well diminish with professional experience. In this way, professional experience could be seen as having a learning effect, contributing to the development of professional wisdom and supporting teachers to develop the ability – and perhaps even confidence – to bring a wider range of considerations to bear on their decision-making and reasoning. This noted, there were two dilemmas, however, where rule-based reasoning was the most popular choice made by participants regardless of career stage: assessment and working with parents.

Furthermore, and as Table 4.1 indicates, there were only two occasions where Experienced Teachers chose the rule-based reason more frequently than the other cohorts: Dilemma 3, Option 2, and Dilemma 6, Option 2. These dilemmas share a common feature: they involved potential conflict with colleagues. One conclusion drawn in *The Good Teacher* study was that Experienced Teachers may rely on rules-based reasoning in situations concerning working relationships with their colleagues.

Table 4.1 Percentage of Participants Who Selected the Rule-Based Answer, by Career Stage

	Di1 Op1	*Di1 Op2*	*Di2 Op1*	*Di2 Op2*	*Di3 Op1*	*Di3 Op2*	*Di4 Op1*	*Di4 Op2*	*Di5 Op1*	*Di5 Op2*	*Di6 Op1*	*Di6 Op2*	*Di6 Op3*
Student Teachers	7	12	22	3	67	26	48	52	22	5	20	14	3
NQTs	5	11	18	7	11	25	25	55	19	4	2	21	3
Experienced Teachers	2	11	21	4	0	27	15	45	19	0	4	39	3

The dilemma that produced the lowest percentage of rule-based reasoning (for either possible course of action) was the dilemma concerning curriculum flexibility in which students were asking to go out in the snow. For this dilemma, respondents were more confident in basing this decision on the virtues of creativity, curiosity and love of learning. With these reflections in mind, a suggestion offered by *The Good Teacher* study is that there may be a connection between drawing on rule-based reasoning and the extent to which the key protagonist (the teacher) is in a 'high-stakes' situation (practices concerning assessment, judgements about the professionalism of colleagues, dealing with parents) or a situation in which there may be scope – whether real or perceived – for greater freedom to exercise professional judgement and autonomy.

Conclusion

The data presented and analysed in this chapter provides an indication of how teachers at different stages of their career perceive their personal character strengths as teachers and the character strengths equated with the 'ideal' or 'good' teacher. Noting their different respondent groups and sets of 24 character strengths utilised, both *The Good Teacher* data and the *Teacher Education* data provide some evidence that as teachers progress through their career, and as student teachers progress through their initial teacher education programme, different emphases on character strengths can be identified. In regard to the dilemma data, as we suggested in Chapter 1, while rules clearly play a role in guiding teachers' ethical professional practice, teachers typically also draw on a range of other considerations – including virtue-based justifications. Of further interest here, however, is the analysis of the dilemma data offered within *The Good Teacher* report that makes the tentative suggestion that the extent to which teachers draw on/prioritise virtue-based reasoning may be influenced by the sort of dilemma faced. More specifically, the data raises the possibility that a connection may exist between drawing on rule-based reasoning and salient situational factors that are deemed by the teacher to be 'high-stakes' situation (practices concerning assessment, judgements about the professionalism of colleagues, dealing with parents) or a situation in which there may be scope – whether real or perceived – for greater freedom to exercise professional judgement and autonomy. As is set out in the conclusion which follows, this tentative finding indicates a need for further research.

Notes

1 www.viacharacter.org/character-strengths.
2 Seven character strengths are reported for the post survey as confidence and resourcefulness both had a ranking of 6.5%.
3 ($p = 0.09 < \alpha\ 0.1$) 90% confidence level.
4 The process by which the Expert Panel was formed, and its role in the research, can be found in Appendix One.

Conclusion, recommendations and further research

Introduction

As stated from the outset, and as with the wider work of the Jubilee Centre, this book and the studies contained within it are premised on the idea that what constitutes a 'good' teacher necessarily involves more than technical skills and subject knowledge. A good teacher not only appreciates and embraces the ethical dimensions of their role but also understands the various actors, policies, practices and pressures that impact on how that role is shaped and enacted. Teachers – as with other professionals – work in increasingly challenging times; many competing demands are placed upon teachers and the teaching profession generally. With this in mind, teachers must be supported to develop their professional judgement and wisdom in order to respond to the ethical demands of their work. This does not mean that teachers do, or indeed should, operate as autonomous individuals. Teachers form part of wider networks, whether within schools, the local community or wider society. In other words, while some given situations may require teachers to make a decision as an individual teacher, in reality teachers act interdependently with others in discharging their ethical role.

In the preceding two chapters, various aspects of this ethical role have been explored from the perspectives of teachers themselves. In this closing chapter, we draw together the overall findings from the three projects – *The Good Teacher, Teacher Education* and *Schools of Virtue* – before offering several recommendations and identifying some fertile areas in need of further research.

Overall findings

Here we present, adapt and extend the findings of the three project reports drawn on in this book (Arthur et al., 2015a, 2017, 2018a):

- Teachers recognise and appreciate the moral nature of their work, understanding themselves as having a role to play in educating for character. Teachers affirm the positive impact that developing character can have on pupils and on key relationships within the school. They saw character education not only as integral to their teaching but also as something that happens through extra-curricular activities and with the help of role models.

- Teachers had high expectations of the difference they can make with children, driven by a love of their subject, a natural enthusiasm to inspire young people in education and a desire to work with those young people.
- Teachers at various careers stages reported certain character strengths as being of more importance than others. In *The Good Teacher* project, teachers saw fairness, creativity, love of learning, humour, perseverance and leadership as the six most important character strengths for ideal teachers, but in describing their own, personal six most important character strengths, they emphasised kindness and honesty in place of perseverance and leadership. In the *Teacher Education* project, Student Teacher reports on the character strengths of the 'good' teacher emphasised performance and intellectual character strengths. While this conception of the 'good' teacher remained relatively unchanged at the end of the ITE year (in the sense that performance and intellectual character strengths remained emphasised over moral and civic), significant changes occurred to respondents' reported personal character strengths, with a shift to prioritise performance character strengths over moral character strengths. Notably, at the end of the ITE year, Student Teachers' perceptions of their personal character strengths aligned more with their perceptions of the 'good' teacher. Civic character strengths were consistently the least emphasised.
- Again in *The Good Teacher* project, when asked to consider a set of moral dilemmas, teachers drew upon virtue-based reasoning considerably, especially in areas of moral or practical significance. Yet, rule-based reasoning dominated in specific cases – such as assessment – where rules are clear-cut and reflect overall political and professional trends in teaching. Experienced Teachers chose rule-based reasoning less frequently than teachers at earlier stages of their careers, the exception being where conflict with colleagues was involved.
- While notions such as the desire to 'make a difference to children's lives' often motivated teachers to enter the profession, teachers expressed concern about the impact of policy and workload on maintaining the passion and enthusiasm for teaching they felt at the start of their careers. For example, workload pressures were

cited as reducing the time and energy teachers had for reflection on their personal motivations and the kind of teacher and moral exemplar that they wished to be. The relevance of this finding is further emphasised when considered in relation to a recent Jubilee Centre research study examining the ethical across professions (Arthur et al., 2019a: 10). Drawing on data from 2,340 professionals, the study found that 'regardless of stage of career, practitioners valuing character reported greater experiences of "good" professional purpose compared to groups that devalued character'.
- Where workload and other pressures acted negatively on teachers' motivations and ability to assume their moral role, supportive colleagues and environments provided important mechanisms to help teachers to meet the demands they faced.
- The data suggested that university teacher education provides an important theoretical and pedagogical context for reflecting on classroom practice. Learning by example from role models who are good mentors is important. However, the quality of mentoring and preparation for character education seem to be variable.
- In *The Good Teacher* project, Teacher Educators reported that character matters in teaching. However, this seemed to be based on particular conceptions of character that centred on performance rather than moral virtues. This focus on performance virtues encouraged a focus on the superficial aspects of professional practice, such as dress and behaviour, at the expense of deeper reflection on the personal virtues needed for good teaching.

Overall recommendations

With these overall findings in mind, we draw on and extend on the recommendations contained within the three project reports to propose the following overall recommendations:

- The shift in educational emphasis from character to technical competency and subject knowledge, and from teacher professionalism to accountability, needs to be realigned. What it means to be a 'good' teacher needs be rooted in wider visualisations of what education is for and what human characteristics need to be developed, and why. These visualisations should receive explicit attention from policy makers, school leaders, teachers and teacher educators.

- While it is important that teachers understand and appreciate the ethical nature of the teaching profession, teachers must be supported to do so. Whether from government, senior leaders, governors, parents or the wider community, teachers and the teaching profession need continued support and recognition for the work they do to make a difference to pupils' lives, including developing character.
- Given its potential impact on shaping how beginning teachers conceive what it means to be a 'good' teacher, initial teacher education should focus on developing the moral agency of teachers, resisting the tendency to adhere to a reductive, formulaic model of teaching and making explicit the moral language of teaching. Making space for ethical reflection on practice and developing understanding of character education are two key priorities in this regard.
- Similarly, there needs to be a greater recognition of the moral importance of mentoring and coaching in teaching. Schools need to ensure that teachers have time in their workloads to allow for the proper development of mentoring and coaching through good quality training and shared critical understandings of moral and practical excellence.
- Insofar as the Teacher Educators have conceptualised character in teaching in terms of rule-governed 'professional' behaviour, teacher education should include academic input and deliberative reflection concerning the role of *moral* virtues in teaching and the teaching profession today.
- While examining moral character should form a core part of pre-service initial teacher education, an emphasis on moral character is important throughout teachers' careers and needs to be reflected in CPD programmes to ensure that momentum is maintained and the early enthusiasm of teachers wanting to make a difference is sustained.
- Academics, teachers and teacher educators may benefit from considering the nature of civic virtues, and the extent to which civic virtues are, or indeed are not, important to the professional work of teachers.

Future research

The analysis of data presented in this book raises a myriad of possible trajectories and emphases for future research. To extend current understandings of what constitutes 'the good teacher', the following are particularly relevant:

- While the data analysed in the project reported in this book focused on teachers at particular stages of their professional career, further longitudinal research tracking the same teacher(s) over a sustained period of time are likely to obtain a deeper sense of the trajectories and nuances of being a 'good' teacher, including the ethical dimensions of the profession.
- Given the importance of leadership styles and cultures, further research is needed that investigates how different styles of leadership in educational environments impact on teachers' understandings, commitment and enactment of their moral role.
- On the basis that not all aspects of the 'good' teacher are in and of themselves moral, we need to know more about how other features of the 'good' teacher, such as disciplinary subject knowledge, connect with the ethical basis of teaching.
- Given that the research presented in this book, and other research focusing more specifically on teacher well-being, suggests that collaborative and supportive working relationships within schools sustain motivation and commitment to the teaching profession, it is important that the role of such working relationships in aiding the ethical dimensions of teaching is paid more attention within and through empirical research.
- Despite a reasonably widespread acceptance that character development *does* connect with other educational goals, surprisingly little empirical evidence exists that explores the relationship between character education and subject expertise, positive behaviour, improved attainment and employability. These relationships require further investigation.
- While the three studies have all been undertaken on the understanding that the implementation of character education by school leaders and teachers must be informed and guided by the particular contexts, needs and communities of individual schools, more empirical evidence is needed about what this actually means in practice. In particular, while the *Schools of Virtue* project undertook case studies in three schools, more in-depth case studies are needed both to provide insights across a wider range of contexts and to also enable meaningful meta-analysis of these case studies to take place.
- Given that the dilemma data in *The Good Teacher* project seemed to suggest a connection between the type of dilemma faced (high

or low stakes, involving a colleague or not, for example) and the prioritisation of certain types of justification (rule-based or virtue-based, for example), further research with teachers utilising dilemmas is needed to test whether such connections can be identified and to examine possible explanations.

- At a time when concerns have been expressed about (dis)connections between schools and the 'public' good, further research is needed to examine whether, and if so how, teachers conceive themselves as 'public' professionals contributing to the common good of society.

Appendices

Appendix One: the expert panel process

Stage 1: **First meeting with expert panel:**

- Introduction to the project and its aims
- Introduction to the VIA 24 character strengths
- Examples of SJT's used to assess ethical judgement in professionals context (e.g. EHCI, Rezlar...)
- Brainstorming exercise of what kinds of dilemmas teachers may experience in their professional practice. These were grouped into categories (e.g. assessment, dealing with parents, enforcing 'unfair' rules etc...)
- Experts then broke into small groups to work on coming up with dilemmas and courses of action which sat within each category.
- The outcome of the first session was four draft dilemmas with a number of draft courses of action.

Stage 2: **Email correspondence with expert panel:**

- A rough draft of the scenarios was prepared, based on the four the panel had devised, and two that they had discussed, but had not got as far as devising. This document was emailed around panel, and they were asked to come to the next meeting having thought about their feedback on the scenarios, and some possible courses of action for each.

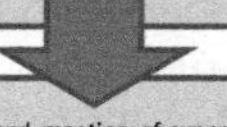

Stage 3: **Second meeting of expert panel:**

- The panel worked through each scenario, clarifying wording and 'realism', then took each scenario in turn as a group to agree 2 or 3 plausible courses of action.
- One scenario was then discussed by the group as a whole, with 5-6 reasons developed for each course of action. These reasons were then mapped onto some of the 24 character strengths to give one 'complete' scenario as a working example.

Stage 4: **Email correspondence with expert panel (2):**

- The six dilemmas and courses of action were prepared, (plus the one fully developed with reasons as an example) in the questionnaire format, and circulated to panel by email
- The panel were each allocated two dilemmas (so each dilemma was worked on by two panel members independently), and asked to come up with 5-6 reasons for each of those dilemma's courses of action, indicating 1 or 2 of the 24 character strengths that their reasons mapped onto. They retuned these by email.
- Reasons were re-sent to the panel in the questionnaire format for their feedback (on the validity/appropriateness of the reasons, and whether they thought these had been mapped onto the correct character strengths).

Stage 5: **Exposure to wider expert audience**

- Once the panel had agreed the scenarios, courses of actions and reasons (and mapped strengths) these were circulated to two meetings of mentors (forty-plus in total) – one internal to the University, one external - to validate the dilemmas and courses of action as plausible, and that the strengths mapped onto the reasons were appropriate.
- The attendees will be sent the dilemmas in the questionnaire format complete in advance of the meeting.

Appendix Two: summary of dilemmas content and associated virtues

Subject area	*Summary of the dilemma*	*Virtues associated with the reasoning by the expert panel*
Curriculum Flexibility	Children wanted to explore the snow during a lesson, where this would disrupt the planned programme, further complicated because for some children snow was a new experience. The teacher had to choose between disrupting the lesson or ignoring the children's requests.	Option 1: Appreciation of beauty; Love of learning; Kindness; Creativity Option 2: Perseverance; Fairness; Leadership
School Rules	A child, Robert, persistently came to school in the wrong shoes but had difficult home circumstances that might have made it difficult for him to afford the regulation ones. The teacher had to choose between sending Robert home or ignoring the trainers.	Option 1: Fairness; Perseverance; Hope; Kindness Option 2: Fairness; Judgement; Perspective; Kindness
Assessment	A junior teacher had to decide whether to join in with her Deputy Head who was helping students with an examination, or to refuse to join in and challenge the senior colleague. Students had been disadvantaged by staff absence earlier in the year.	Option 1: Fairness; Social intelligence; Perspective; Hope Option 2: Fairness; Leadership; Self-regulation; Honesty
Working with Parents	The NQT faced a challenge between maintaining confidentiality at a Parents' Evening or sharing other parents' concerns over distractions posed by a child with Special Educational Needs.	Option 1: Fairness; Honesty; Bravery; Hope Option 2: Prudence; Perspective; Judgement; Kindness
Teaching Sensitive, or Controversial Topics	A student was overheard making apparently racist comments following a citizenship lesson on the 'war on terror'. The teacher had to decide whether to report the child or to tackle the issue in a subsequent lesson with the whole class.	Option 1: Bravery; Prudence; Kindness; Courage Option 2: Judgement; Perspective; Humility; Hope
Relationships with Colleagues	A teacher regularly overheard a colleague making derogatory remarks about a class and commenting that (s)he did not bother preparing properly for their lessons because they were not worth it. The teacher had to choose between ignoring the comments, reporting the colleague or challenging them directly.	Option 1: Self-regulation; Fairness; Judgement; Social intelligence Option 2: Self-regulation; Teamwork; Kindness; Honesty Option 3: Leadership; Bravery; Hope; Prudence

References

Adam, P. (2009) 'Ethics with character: Virtues and the ethical social worker', *The Journal of Sociology & Social Welfare*. 36 (3). 83–105.

Arthur, J. (2003) *Education with Character: The Moral Economy of Schooling*. London: RoutledgeFalmer.

Arthur, J., Davison, J. and Lewis, M. (2005) *Professional Values and Practice: Achieving the Standards for QTS*. Abingdon: Routledge.

Arthur, J. and Revell, L. (2012) *Character Formation in Schools and the Education of Teachers*. Canterbury: Canterbury Christ Church University in partnership with The Esmee Fairbairn Foundation.

Arthur, J., Kristjánsson, K., Thomas, H., Holdsworth, M., Confalonieri, L. B., and Qiu, T. (2014) *Virtuous Character For the Practice of Law*. Birmingham: Jubilee Centre for Character and Virtues, University of Birmingham.

Arthur, J., Kristjánsson, K., Cooke, S., Brown, E. and Carr, D. (2015a) *The Good Teacher: Understanding Virtues in Practice*. Birmingham: Jubilee Centre for Character and Virtues, University of Birmingham.

Arthur, J., Kristjánsson, K., Thomas, H., Kotzee, B., Ignatowicz, A. and Qiu, T. (2015b) *Virtuous Medical Practice*. Birmingham: Jubilee Centre for Character and Virtues, University of Birmingham.

Arthur, J., Kristjánsson, K., Harrison, T., Sanderse, W. and Wright, D. (2016) *Teaching Character and Virtues in Schools*. Abingdon: Routledge.

Arthur, J., Harrison, T., Burn, E. and Moller, F. (2017) *Schools of Virtue: Character Education in Three Birmingham Schools*. Birmingham: Jubilee Centre for Character and Virtues, University of Birmingham.

Arthur, J., Fullard, M., Watts, P. and Moller, F. (2018a) *Character Perspectives of Student Teachers: Initial Insights*. Birmingham: Jubilee Centre for Character and Virtues, University of Birmingham.

Arthur, J., Walker, D. I. and Thoma, S. (2018b) *Soldiers of Character*. Birmingham: Jubilee Centre for Character and Virtues, University of Birmingham.

Arthur, J., Earl, S. R., Thompson, A. P. and Ward, J. W. (2019a) *Repurposing the Professions: The Role of Professional Character – Initial Insights*. Birmingham: Jubilee Centre for Character and Virtues, University of Birmingham.

Arthur, J., Earl, S. R., Thompson, A. P. and Ward, J. W. (2019b) 'The value of character-based judgement in the professional domain', *Journal of Business Ethics*. doi:10.1007/s10551-019-04269-7.

Ball, S. (2003) 'The teachers' soul and the terrors of performativity', *Journal of Education Policy*. 18 (2). 215–228.

Ball, S. (2008) *The Education Debate*. Bristol: Policy Press.

Banks, S. (2003) 'From oaths to rulebooks: A critical examination of codes of ethics for the social professions', *European Journal of Social Work*. 6 (2). 133–144.

Barrett, D. B., Casey, J. E., Visser, R. D. and Headley, K. N. (2012) 'How do teachers make judgements about ethical and unethical behaviours? Towards the development of a code of conduct for teachers', *Teaching and Teacher Education*. 28 (8). 890–898.

Belogolovsky, E. and Somech, A. (2010) 'Teachers' organisational citizenship behaviour: Examining the boundary between in-role behaviour and extra-role behaviour from the perspective of teachers, principals and parents', *Teaching and Teacher Education*. 26. 914–923.

Bessant, J. (2009) 'Aristotle meets youth work: A case for virtue ethics', *Journal of Youth Studies*. 12 (4). 423–438.

Blond, P., Antonacopoulou, E. and Pabst, A. (2015) *In Professions We Trust: Fostering Virtuous Practitioners in Teaching, Law and Medicine*. London: Respublica.

Bohlin, K. (2005) *Teaching Character Education through Literature: Awakening the Moral Imagination in Secondary Classrooms*. London: Routledge.

Boon, H. (2011) 'Raising the bar: Ethics education for quality teachers', *Australian Journal of Teacher Education*. 36. 76–93.

Buzzelli, C. and Johnston, B. (2001) 'Authority, power and morality in classroom discourse', *Teaching and Teacher Education*. 17 (8). 873–884.

Campbell, E. (2008) 'Teaching ethically as a moral condition of professionalism', in L. P. Nucci and D. Narvaez (eds.) *Handbook of Moral and Character Education*. New York: Routledge. pp. 601–618.

Campbell, E. (2000) 'Professional ethics in teaching: towards the development of a code of practice', *Cambridge Journal of Education*. 30 (2). 203–221.

Campbell, E. (2011) 'Teacher education as a missed opportunity in teacher education', in L. Bondi, D. Carr, C. Clark and C. Clegg (eds.) *Towards Professional Wisdom: Practical Deliberation in the People Professions*. Farnham: Ashgate Publishing Company. pp. 81–93.

Campbell, E. (2013) 'The virtuous, wise and knowledgeable teacher: Living the good life as a professional practitioner', *Educational Theory*. 63 (4). 413–430.

Carr, D. (1991) *Educating the Virtues: An Essay on the Philosophical Psychology of Moral Development and Education*. Abingdon: Routledge.

Carr, D. (1993) 'Moral values and the teacher: Beyond the pastoral and the permissive', *Journal of the Philosophy of Education*. 27 (2). 193–227.

Carr, D. (1999) 'Professional education and professional ethics', *Journal of Applied Philosophy*. 16 (1). 33–46.

Carr, D. (2000) *Professionalism and Ethics in Teaching*. Abingdon: Routledge.

Carr, D. (2007) 'Character in teaching', *British Journal of Educational Studies*. 55 (4). 369–389.

Carr, D. (2011) 'Virtue, character and emotion in people professions: Towards a virtue ethics of interpersonal professional conduct', in L. Bondi, D. Carr, C. Clark and C. Clegg (eds.) *Towards Professional Wisdom: Practical Deliberation in the People Professions*. Farnham: Ashgate. pp. 97–110.

Cigman, R. (2000) 'Ethical confidence in education', *Journal of Philosophy of Education*. 34 (4). 643–657.

Colby, A. and Damon, W. (1992) *Some Do Care: Contemporary Lives of Moral Commitment*. New York: The Free Press.

Cooke, S. and Carr, D. (2014) 'Virtue, practical wisdom and character in teaching', *British Journal of Educational Studies*. 62 (2). 91–110.

Coughlan, S. (2018) 'England's schools face 'severe' teaching crisis', *BBC News*. www.bbc.co.uk/news/education-45341734; accessed 18th December 2019.

Cummings, R., Harlow, S. and Maddux, C. D. (2007) 'Moral reasoning of in-service and pre-service teachers: A review of the research', *Journal of Moral Education*. 36 (1). 67–78.

Damon, W. and Colby, A. (2014) *The Power of Ideals: The Real Story of Moral Choice*. New York: Oxford University Press.

Department for Education (2011) *Teachers' Standards*. https://assets.publishing.service.gov.uk/government/uploads/system/uploads/attachment_data/file/665520/Teachers__Standards.pdf; accessed 7th August 2019.

Department for Education (2017) *Developing Character Skills in Schools: Quantitative Survey*. [Online]. Available at: https://assets.publishing.service.gov.uk/government/uploads/system/uploads/attachment_data/file/674231/Developing_Character_skills_survey-report.pdf; accessed 23 August 2018.

De Ruyter, D. J. and Kole, J. J. (2010) 'Our teachers want to be the best: On the necessity of intra-professional reflection about moral ideals of teaching', *Teachers and Teaching: Theory and Practice*. 16 (2). 207–218.

Dishon, G. and Goodman, J. G. (2017) 'No-excuses for character: A critique of character education in no-excuses charter schools', *Theory and Research in Education*. 15 (2). 182–201.

Dixon-Woods, M., Yeung, K. and Bosk, C. L. (2011) 'Why is UK medicine no longer a self-regulating profession? The role of scandals involving "bad apple" doctors', *Social Science & Medicine*. 73 (10). 1452–1459.

Eurofound (2012) *Fifth European Working Conditions Survey*. Luxembourg: Publications Office of the European Union.

Elbaz, F. (1992) 'Hope, Attentiveness, and Caring for Difference: The Moral Voice in Teaching', *Teaching and Teacher Education*. 8 (1). 421–432.

Elliott, J. (1989) 'Teacher evaluation and teaching as a moral science', in M. L. Holly and C. S. McLoughlin (eds.) *Perspectives on Teacher Professional Development*. London: Falmer Press.

Ewing, T. and Manuel, J. (2005) 'Retaining quality early teachers in the profession: New teacher narratives', *Change: Transformations in Education* [Online]. 7 (1). 4–18. Available at: http://ses.library.usyd.edu.au//bitstream/2123/4529/1/Vol8No1Article1.pdf; accessed 19 November 2014.

Fallona, C. (2000) 'Manner in teaching: A study in observing and interpreting teachers' moral virtues', *Teaching and Teacher Education*. 16 (7). 681–695.

Fenstermacher, G. D. (1990) 'Some moral considerations on teaching as a profession', in J. Goodlad, R. Soder and K. A. Sirotnik (eds.) *The Moral Dimensions of Teaching.* San Francisco: Jossey-Bass. pp. 130–154.

Foster, D. (2019) *Teacher Recruitment and Retention in England. Briefing Paper Number 7222.* House of Commons Library. file:///C:/Users/petersoa/Downloads/CBP-7222.pdf; accessed 18th December 2019.

Furlong, W., Crossan, M., Gandz, J. and Crossan, I. (2017) 'Character's essential role in addressing misconduct in financial institutions', *Business Law International.* 18. 199.

Gardner, H., Csikszentmihalyi, M. and Damon, W. (2001) *Good Work: Where Excellence and Ethics Meet.* New York: Basic Books.

Glaser, B. G. and Strauss, A. L. (1967) *The Discovery of Grounded Theory: Strategies for Qualitative Research.* New York: Aldine de Gruyter.

Goodfellow, J. (2003) 'Practical wisdom in professional practice: The person in the process', *Contemporary Issues in Early Childhood.* 4 (1). 48–63.

Green, J. (2011) *Education, Professionalism and the Quest for Accountability.* Abingdon: Routledge.

Hand, M. (2018) *A Theory of Moral Education.* Abingdon: Routledge.

Hansen, D. (2001) *Exploring the Moral Heart of Teaching: Towards a Teacher's Creed.* New York: Pearson.

Harrison, T., Arthur, J. and Burn, E. (eds.) (2016) *Character Education Evaluation Handbook for Schools.* Birmingham: Jubilee Centre for Character and Virtues, University of Birmingham. Available at: http://www.jubileecentre.ac.uk/1721/character-education/resources/evaluation-handbook-for-schools; accessed 20th November 2019.

Harrison, T., Morris, I. and Ryan, J. (2016) *Teaching Character in the Primary Classroom.* London: Sage.

Harrison, T. and Khatoon, B. (2017) *Virtue, Practical Wisdom and Professional Education: A Pilot Intervention Designed to Enhance Virtue Knowledge, Understanding and Reasoning in Student Lawyers, Doctors and Teachers.* Birmingham: Jubilee Centre for Character and Virtues, University of Birmingham.

Harrison, T. and Walker, D. I. (2018) *The Theory and Practice of Virtue Education.* Abingdon: Routledge.

Hendrikx, W. (2019) 'What we should do vs what we do: Teachers' professional identity in a context of managerial reform', *Educational Studies.* doi: 10.1080/03055698.2019.1620694.

Higgins, C. (2001) 'From reflective practice to practical wisdom: Three models of liberal teacher education', *Philosophy of Education.* 2. 92–99.

Hinds, D. (2019) *Education Secretary Sets Out Five Foundations to Build Character.* https://www.gov.uk/government/speeches/education-secretary-sets-out-five-foundations-to-build-character; accessed 9th September 2019.

Holbeche, L. and Springett, N. (2004) '*In Search of Meaning at Work*', Roffey Park Institute, Horsham. http://citeseerx.ist.psu.edu/viewdoc/download?doi=10.1.1.458.1538&rep=rep1&type=pdf; accessed 18th May 2018.

Husu, J. and Tirri, K. (2003) 'A case study approach to study one teacher's moral reflection', *Teaching and Teacher Education.* 19 (3). 345–357.

Husu, J. and Tirri, K. (2007) 'Developing Whole School Pedagogical Values – A Case of Going through the Ethos of 'Good Schooling'', *Teaching and Teacher Education*. 23 (4). 390–401.

Jubilee Centre for Character and Virtues (2017) *A Framework for Character Education in Schools*. Birmingham: Jubilee Centre for Character and Virtues, University of Birmingham. https://www.jubileecentre.ac.uk/userfiles/jubileecentre/pdf/character-education/Framework%20for%20Character%20Education.pdf; accessed 14th August 2019.

Kidger, J., Brockman, R., Tilling, K., Campbell, R., Ford, T., Araya, R., King, M. and Gunnell, D. (2016) 'Teachers' wellbeing and depressive symptoms, and associated risk factors: A large cross sectional study in English secondary schools', *Journal of Affective Disorders*. 192. 76–82.

Kinsella, E. A. and Pitman, A. (2012) 'Engaging phronesis in professional practice and education', in E. A. Kinsella and A. Pitman (eds.) *Phronesis as Professional Knowledge: Practical Wisdom in the Professions*. Rotterdam: Sense. pp. 1–13.

Kotzee, B., Paton, A. and Conroy, M. (2016) 'Towards an empirically informed account of *phronesis* in medicine', *Perspectives in Biology and Medicine*. 59 (3). 337–350.

Kristjánsson, K. (2013) 'Ten myths about character, virtue and virtue education – Plus three well-founded misgivings', *British Journal of Educational Studies*. 61 (3). 269–287.

Kristjánsson, K. (2015a) *Aristotelian Character Education*. Abingdon: Routledge.

Kristjánsson, K. (2015b) 'Phronesis as an ideal in professional medical ethics: Some preliminary positionings and problematics', *Theoretical Medicine and Bioethics*. 36 (5). 299–320.

Kristjánsson, K., Thomas, H., Kotzee, B., Ignatowicz, A. and Qiu, T. (2015) *Virtuous Medical Practice*. Birmingham: Jubilee Centre for Character and Virtues, University of Birmingham.

Kristjánsson, K., Arthur, J., Moller, F. and Huo, Y. (2017a) *Character and Virtues in Business and Finance*. Birmingham: Jubilee Centre for Character and Virtues, University of Birmingham.

Kristjánsson, K., Varghese, J., Arthur, J. and Moller, F. with Ferkany, M. (2017b) *Virtuous Practice in Nursing*. Birmingham: Jubilee Centre for Character and Virtues, University of Birmingham.

Ladd, J. (1998) 'The quest for a code of ethics: An intellectual and moral confusion', in P. Vesilund and A. Gunn (eds.) *Engineering, Ethics and the Environment*. Cambridge: Cambridge University Press. pp. 210–218.

Lewis, C. S. (1985) *Letters to Children*. New York: MacMillan.

LoCasale-Crouch, J., Davis, E., Wiens, P. and Pianta, R. (2012) 'The role of the mentor in supporting new teachers: Associations with self-efficacy, reflection, and quality', *Mentoring and Tutoring: Partnership in Learning*. 20 (3). 303–323.

Loonstra, B., Brouwers, A. and Tomic, W. (2009) 'Feelings of existential fulfilment and burnout among secondary school teachers', *Teaching and Teacher Education*. 25. 752–757.

Mahoney, P. (2009) 'Should 'ought' be taught?', *Teaching and Teacher Education*. 25. 983–989.

Manuel, J. and Hughes, J. (2006) 'It has always been my dream: Exploring pre-service teachers' motivations for choosing to teach', *Teacher Development: An International Journal of Teachers' Professional Development*. 10 (1). 5–24.

Maxwell, B. and Schwimmer, M. (2016) 'Professional ethics education for future teachers: A narrative review of the scholarly writings', *Journal of Moral Education*. 45 (3). 354–371.

McKie, A., Baguley, F., Guthrie, C., Jackson, C., Kirkpatrick, P., Laing, A., O'Brien, S., Taylor, R. and Wimpenny, P. (2012) 'Exploring clinical wisdom in nursing education', *Nursing Ethics*. 19 (2). 252–267.

Morgan, N. (2014) *Speech at the Conservative Party Conference 2014*, 28 September – 01 October 2014, Conservative Conference 2014, Birmingham, [Online]. Available at: http://press.conservatives.com/post/98807929855/nicky-morgan-speech-to-conservative-party; accessed 14th August 2019.

Oakley, J. and Cocking, D. (2001) *Virtue Ethics and Professional Roles*. Cambridge: Cambridge University Press.

Office for Standards in Education (2019a) *Teacher Well-being at Work in Schools and Further Education Providers*. https://assets.publishing.service.gov.uk/government/uploads/system/uploads/attachment_data/file/819314/Teacher_well-being_report_110719F.pdf; accessed 9th September 2019.

Office for Standards in Education (2019b) *The Education Inspection Framework*. https://assets.publishing.service.gov.uk/government/uploads/system/uploads/attachment_data/file/801429/Education_inspection_framework.pdf; accessed 9th September 2019.

Osguthorpe, R. D. (2008) 'On the reasons we want teachers of good disposition and moral character', *Journal of Teacher Education*. 59. 288–299.

Osguthorpe, R. and Sanger, M. (2013) 'Teacher candidate beliefs about the moral work of teaching', in M. Sanger and R. Osguthorpe (eds.) *The Moral Work of Teaching and Teacher Education. Preparing and Supporting Practitioners*. New York, London: Teachers College Press. pp. 14–27.

Pellegrino, E. D. and Thomasma, D. C. (1993) *The Virtues in Medical Practice*. New York: Oxford University Press.

Perryman, J. and Calvert, G. (2019) 'What motivates people to teach, and why do they leave? Accountability, performativity and teacher retention', *British Journal of Educational Studies*. doi:10.1080/00071005.2019.1589417.

Peterson, C. and Seligman, M. (2004) *Character Strengths and Virtues: A Handbook and Classification*. Washington: Oxford University Press.

Peterson, C. and Park, N. (2009) 'Classifying and measuring strengths of character', in S. J. Lopez and C. R. Snyder (eds.) *Oxford Handbook of Positive Psychology*. New York: Oxford University Press. pp. 25–34.

Peterson, A. and Bentley, B. (2017) 'Education for citizenship in South Australian public schools: A pilot study of senior leader and teacher perceptions', *The Curriculum Journal*. 28 (1). 105–122.

Pietarinen, J., Pyhälto, K., Soini, T. and Salmela-Aro, K. (2013) 'Reducing teacher burnout: A socio-cultural approach', *Teaching and Teacher Education*. 35. 62–72.

Pitman, A. (2012) 'Professionalism and professionalization: Hostile ground for growing phronesis', in E. A. Kinsella and A. Pitman (eds.) *Phronesis as Professional Knowledge: Practical Wisdom in the Professions*. Rotterdam: Sense. pp. 131–146.

Richter, D., Kunter, M., Lüdtke, O., Klusmann, U., Anders, Y. and Baumert, J. (2013) 'How different mentoring approaches affect beginning teachers' development in the first years of practice', *Teaching and Teacher Education*. 36. 166–167.

Ritchie, J. and Spencer, L. (1994) 'Qualitative data analysis for applied policy research', in A. Bryman and R. G. Burgess (eds.) *Analyzing Qualitative Data*. London: Routledge. pp. 173–194.

Royal Pharmaceutical Society (2011) *Reducing Workplace Pressure through Professional Empowerment*. https://www.rpharms.com/Portals/0/RPS%20document%20library/Open%20access/Support/64585_Reducing%20Workplace%20Pressure%20through%20professional%20empowerment%20-%20FINAL.PDF?ver=2017-05-16-133220-000; accessed 20th November 2019.

Sanderse, W. and Cooke, S. (2019) 'Being prepared to become a moral teacher: UK teachers' experiences of initial teacher education', *Scandinavian Journal of Educational Research*. doi:10.1080/00313831.2019.1664628.

Sanger, M. and Osguthorpe, R. D. (2011) `Teacher Education, Pre-service Teacher Beliefs and the Moral Work of Teaching', *Teaching and Teacher Education*. 27 (3), 569–578.

Sanger, M. N. and Osguthorpe, R. D. (2013) 'Modelling as moral education: Documenting, analysing, and addressing a central belief of pre-service teachers', *Teaching and Teacher Education*. 29. 167–176.

Schwartz, B. (2009) 'Our loss of wisdom', *TED2009*. https://www.ted.com/talks/barry_schwartz_our_loss_of_wisdom?; accessed 24th November 2019.

Schwartz, B. (2011) 'Using our practical wisdom', *TEDSalon New York*. https://www.ted.com/talks/barry_schwartz_using_our_practical_wisdom?language=en; accessed 24th November 2019.

Schwartz, B. (2014) Why a good teacher must be a wise teacher. The Jubilee Centre for Character and Virtues: Insight Series. https://www.jubileecentre.ac.uk/userfiles/jubileecentre/pdf/insight-series/SchwartzB.pdf; accessed 14th August 2019.

Schwimmer, M. and Maxwell, B. (2017) 'Codes of ethics and teacher's professional autonomy', *Ethics and Education*. 12 (2). 141–152.

See, B-H. and Gorard, S. (2019) 'Why don't we have enough teachers?: A reconsideration of the available evidence', *Research Papers in Education*. doi: 10.1080/02671522.2019.1568535.

Seider, S. (2012) *Character Compass*. Cambridge, MA: Harvard Education Press.

Seijts, G., Crossan, M. and Carleton, E. (2017) 'Embedding leader character into HR practices and to achieve sustained excellence', *Organizational Dynamics*. 44 (1). 65–74.

Sellman, D. (2009) 'Practical wisdom in health and social care: Teaching for professional phronesis', *Learning in Health and Social Care*. 8 (2). 84–91.

Sellman, D. (2012) 'Reclaiming competence for professional phronesis', in E. A. Kinsella and A. Pitman (eds.) *Phronesis as Professional Knowledge: Practical Wisdom in the Professions*. Rotterdam: Sense. pp. 115–130.

Shapira-Lishchinsky, O. (2009) 'Towards professionalism: Ethical perspectives of Israeli teachers', *European Journal of Teacher Education*. 32 (4). 473–487.

Skaalvik, E. M. and Skaalvik, S. (2010) 'Teacher self-efficacy and teacher burnout: A study of relations', *Teaching and Teacher Education*. 24 (4). 1059–1069.

Skaalvik, E. M. and Skaalvik, S. (2011) 'Teachers' feeling of belonging, exhaustion, and job satisfaction: The role of school goal structure and value consonance', *Anxiety, Stress, and Coping*. 24 (4). 369–387.

Sockett, H. and LePage, P. (2002) 'The missing language of the classroom', *Teaching and Teacher Education*. 18. 159–171.

Sockett, H. (2012) *Knowledge and Virtue in Teaching and Learning: The Primacy of Dispositions*. New York: Routledge.

Strike, K. A. and Soltis, J. F. (1985) *The Ethics of Teaching*. New York: Teachers College Press.

Strike, K. A. and Soltis, J. F. (2009) *The Ethics of Teaching, 5th Edition*. New York: Teachers College Press.

Thomson, M. M., Turner, J. E. and Nietfield, J. L. (2012) 'A typological approach to investigate the teaching career decision: Motivations and beliefs about teaching of prospective teacher candidates', *Teaching and Teacher Education*. 28 (3). 324–335.

Tom, A. R. (1984) *Teaching as a Moral Craft*. New York: Longman.

Tomlinson, S. (2001) *Education in a Post-Welfare Society*. Buckingham: Oxford University Press.

Ulvik, M., Smith, K. and Helleve, I. (2017) 'Ethical aspects of professional dilemmas in the first year of teaching', *Professional Development in Education*. 43 (2). 236–252.

Walsh, L. and Casinader, N. (2019) 'Investigating the moral territories of international education: A study of the impact of experience, perspectives and dispositions on teachers' engagement with difference in the International Baccalaureate Primary Years Programme', *International Research in Geographical and Environmental Education*. 28 (2). 136–150.

West, A. (2017) 'The ethics of professional accountants: An Aristotelian perspective', *Accounting, Auditing & Accountability Journal*. 30 (2). 328–351.

Wilson, J. (1993) *Reflection and Practice: Teacher Education and the Teaching Profession*. London, Ontario: Althouse Press.

Worth, J. and Van Den Brande, J. (2019) *Teacher Labour Market in England: Annual Report 2019*. https://www.nfer.ac.uk/media/3344/teacher_labour_market_in_england_2019.pdf; accessed 20th November 2019.

Index

Note: **Bold** page numbers refer to tables; *italic* page numbers refer to figures and charts.